CHARLES G. KOONITZ

TECHNICAL ANALYSIS

FOR BEGINNERS PART ONE

Stop Blindly Following Stock Picks of Wall Street's Gurus and Learn Technical Analysis

THIRD EDITION

Copyright © 2018 by Charles G. Koonitz. All rights reserved.

Published by Tripod Solutions Inc.

No part of this book may be reproduced, stored in a retrieval system, or transmitted in any form or by any other means, electronic, mechanical, photocopying, recording, or otherwise, without the prior written express permission of the publisher and copyright owner. Unauthorized duplication of this material in any form is strictly prohibited. Lawbreakers will be prosecuted to the fullest extent of the jurisprudence. Technical Analysis for Beginners Part One and Part Two is sold exclusively on Amazon. Any other seller of this book will be prosecuted.

The limit of liability/disclaimer of warranty: The advice and strategies contained herein may not be suitable for your situation. You should consult a professional where appropriate. Neither the publisher nor author shall be liable for any loss of profit or any other commercial damages, including but not limited to special, incidental, consequential, or other damages.

Charts generated with BigCharts.com, FreeStockCharts.com, and Stockcharts.com

Follow Koonitz:

Twitter: @JumpyStocks

Book and Cover design by Koonitz

ISBN: 978-1-989118-06-1 Paperback color

ISBN : 978-1-989118-13-9 Paperback black & white

ISBN: 978-1-989118-08-5 Ebook

Third edition: July 2018

TABLE OF CONTENTS

PREFACE .... **vii**

INTRODUCTION **1**

Who Can Be Trusted? 1

Make Your Own Research 1

Tough Financial Markets 1

Legend 2

Chapter 1 – What is Technical Analysis? **3**

Type of Charts 4

Candlesticks in Detail 4

Chapter 2 – Preliminary Analysis **9**

Chapter 3 – The Trend **11**

A Simple Tool 13

Support and Resistance 15

Trend Channel 18

Divergence 19

Chapter 4 – Recognizing Breakout **21**

Breakout 21

Breakdown 23

Channel Break 24
Short Selling 25

Chapter 5 – Trend Indicators 27

Simple Moving Average (SMA) 27
The Strategy of Crossing Moving Averages 29
Exponential Moving Average (EMA) 31
Moving Average Convergence Divergence (MACD) 32
Average Directional Index (ADX) 34
Parabolic SAR 35
Force Index 36

Chapter 6 – Momentum Indicators 39

Stochastic 39
Relative Strength Index (RSI) 41
Rate of Change (ROC) 42
Chaikin Money Flow 43

Chapter 7 – Volatility Indicators 45

Bollinger Bands 45
Average True Range (ATR) 46

Chapter 8 – Volume Indicators 49

Volume 49
Intraday Volume 50
Volume by Price 51
Accumulation/Distribution 52
On Balance Volume (OBV) 53

Chapter 9 – Continuation Patterns 55

Cup and Handle 55
Dead-Cat Bounce 56
Triangle – Ascending Triangle 58
Triangle – Descending Triangle 60
Bull Flag and Pennant 61
Bear Flag and Pennant 63

Bullish or Falling Wedge....64
Bearish or Rising Wedge....65

Chapter 10 – Reversal Patterns.... 67

Bump and Run Reversal Bottom....68
Bump and Run Reversal Top....69
Double and Triple Bottom....70
Double and Triple Top....71
Head-and-Shoulders Bottom....72
Head-and-Shoulders Top....73
Rounding Bottom....75
The Parabolic Rise....76

Chapter 11 – Candlesticks Patterns.... 79

Chapter 12 – Avoid the Traps.... 87

Fibonacci Retracement....87
Fake Head-and-Shoulders....88
No Trend at All....88
Adjust Your Moving Averages....89
Risky Symmetrical Triangle....90
Another Risky Symmetrical Triangle....90
Super Rocket Stock....91
Long Candles & Long Shadows....92

Chapter 13 – Trading Psychology.... 93

Avoid Emotional Pitfalls....93
Take Control of Your Emotions....94
The Market Cycle of Emotions....95
Be Disciplined....96

Chapter 14 – Analysis of a Stock.... 97

Weekly Chart Settings....97
How to Analyze a Weekly Chart....98
Daily Chart Settings....99
How to Analyze a Daily Chart....99

Chapter 15 – An Upward Day 101

Chapter 16 – Stock Market Gurus 103

Choosing a Guru 103

Be Cautious About Gurus 104

CONCLUSION 105

GLOSSARY 107

BIBLIOGRAPHY 111

INDEX 113

PREFACE

Many people can be seen discussing capital markets, but only a few of them are actively involved in investment decisions. Instead, people prefer to let professionals make the right decisions. The words **Technical Analysis** scare away many people who believe that it is laboratory analysis using complex mathematical formulas. It's wrong.

This book is the result of my trading experiences since 1996, an extraordinary time when the appearance of the web has upset a whole generation. At this time, we were witnessing the emergence of the charting and trading platforms. Like any beginner who wants to get into action quickly, I have invested naively without worrying about the cruel reality of the markets.

From that moment, I surrounded myself with experienced investors who taught me basic knowledge to secure my approach. Knowing that it is possible to analyze something other than the price curve was, for me, an extraordinary revelation. Anybody can make investment decisions based on indicators, patterns, and divergences. From this day forward, no transaction will be made without first having made a serious analysis.

Having worked in the world of information technology, I had to prepare many training materials useful to future users. It was from that moment that I went into the publishing world to produce my own books. This book contains basic information for the novice who wants to become familiar with the field. The book is filled with graphics and color charts plus simple comments. Forget about magic formulas; technical analysis requires only a sense of observation.

INTRODUCTION

The other day, I was chatting with a friend, and he told me a story similar to the one I had heard several times before. A young man had placed all his savings, about $20,000, on a single stock, after the advice of his father. The latter had mentioned that Affimax could not do anything but go up because the stock had already lost 50% of its value.

On November 17, 2012, Affimax indeed reached a high of $27.74. On February 13, 2013, the stock closed at $16.91. On February 14, the stock fell 31% at opening to $11.60, but it bounced back and closed at $15.74. That same day, in the morning, the well-meaning father advised his son to invest in that stock because he thought that it had reached an incredibly low limit. It would only bounce back up from there. The son invested the $20,000 following the advice of his father at an average cost of $15.35 per share, for a total of 1,300 shares.

Figure 0.1: Bad Call

From February 15 to 22, 2013, the stock remained rather stable at $16.36. On February 25, following the weekend, the massacre happened. The stock fell violently and closed at $2.42, with the young man registering an unbelievable loss of $16,809. On April 18, the initial investment is worth only $1,326 compared to $20,000. Even the best chartist couldn't fully predict that one of the company's drugs would lead to the death of three patients. The product was pulled out of the market, and the stock lost 85% of its value in a single day. This exceptional situation brings out an important element: too many investors blindly take the advice of their friends, their gurus or those close to them, without having any knowledge about their investment.

Who Can Be Trusted?

This book does not intend to prevent you from trying the many stock market gurus you can find across the web. We can't deny that it may be interesting to follow the recommendations of a guru. Many are well connected with the market. Some of them have the flair, while others have research teams that do the technical work. However, you should know that a large number of those gurus have only very slight knowledge about technical analysis. Many of their recommendations are based on simple impulses or on fundamental stock analysis.

For a short-term or medium-term investor, the fundamental analysis is less important. The fundamental analysis allows you to evaluate a company through accounting, financial and strategic analysis, which can rank it in comparison to its competitors. It also allows evaluating the development perspective according to market forces such as supply, demand and technological innovation. Fundamental analysis is perfect for those who have long-term objectives, wishing to build a stable investment portfolio.

Many gurus spend their days in front of their screens. Often enough, their strategy consists of searching for a small gain from $250 to $300 for an investment of $5,000 to $10,000. As soon as they are positioned, they announce the new selection to their subscribers. As you cannot be connected in real time to their transactions, you cannot obtain the return that the 'masters' obtain. I believe you can't win by using this strategy. There's another point worth considering. Starting from the moment they announce their picks to their subscribers, some gurus are ready to sell what they've just recommended as a good buy. It's the same for the big banks. Their specialists provide us with recommendations, some of them quite questionable, which begin to resemble a marketing campaign.

More than anything, this book intends to allow newbie investors to assimilate some knowledge that will come in handy when it's time to buy or sell a financial stock. Trusting the advanced knowledge of a trading guru might be useful, but you should always do your homework and take a look at the chart of the stock suggested. Stay away from pump-and-dump schemes. And you, what kind of investor are you? What inspires you? Is it the day trading, the swing trading or the long-term investment? If you still want to choose a guru, it is up to you to find one who corresponds to your trading style and your availability. So, you want to be a day trader? Are you working during the daytime? Forget it! Choose a guru who works in harmony with your trading style and your lifestyle.

When you shop for a new vehicle, you take the time to examine the various products offered to you. You do some research, look at magazines and do some road tests. It's normal when you're investing $30,000 in a vehicle. So why not do it when you invest in the stock exchange? The beginning of my introduction has demonstrated something fundamental: it's necessary to avoid blindly trusting a colleague, a friend or a member of your family when it's time to invest in a financial stock. So, be careful when choosing your guru. Before trading, analyze the guru's recommendations to see if they seem to be quality ones. If your guru is safe, he will suggest good stocks every week. In that case, no need to run.

Make Your Own Research

You should do some research on each financial stock before investing. To help you with your research, I strongly recommend Yahoo! Finance, which offers all the necessary information for the analysis of your stock. Here is the minimum information you need to get:

- The ticker of the company
- The sector of the company
- The stock market capitalization
- The number of employees
- The competitors
- The high and low for the current year
- The date of the next quarterly results release
- The American, European and Asian market trends

I'm not minimizing the importance of a guru but instead recommending that you understand and master technical analysis before anything else. It's the only way to validate the picks suggested by your specialist. You should always do the technical analysis of the stock you want to buy in order to see if it's in good shape. All the examples of this book are based on past situations and are well documented. This book requires some technical knowledge. It addresses newbie investors who want to get to the heart of the matter faster.

Tough Financial Markets

We must recognize that financial markets are much more complex than they were 20 years ago. The introduction of computers and trading platforms has changed the portrait of the small investor. Anyone with Internet access can now transact electronically on the American, European and Asian markets. Brokerage firms and banks will welcome you with open arms.

If the arrival of the personal computer has democratized trading, clearly it has not allowed the average investor to profit more than they did in the 20th century. Banks and investment companies took control over the market by exercising the High-Frequency Trading (HFT), manipulating the LIBOR rate and the price of natural resources. In addition, products such as commercial paper and Exchange-Traded Funds (ETF) came and denatured stock markets with more than questionable products.

The markets have not finished launching false signals. While it is believed to be in a position to break out to reap handsome profits, the share price quickly converges downward, caused by sales done in less than one millisecond. If the trader is better served there than 20 years ago, know the banks and financial firms still have more power than you think.

Technical analysis is far from an exact science. However, it is the only tool you have to plan your buying and selling decisions. Figures, patterns, and moving averages crossings are indicators that are scrutinized by all stakeholders. It is for this reason that markets appear to respond in unison when a new buy or sell signal emerges. To profit, we must find the means to act early, at the beginning of a bull market.

There are dozens of indicators to monitor the markets. Each year, minor mathematical geniuses generate new formulas. Make no mistake, the indicators are based on interchangeable variables: price, volume, time and other factors such as the Fibonacci sequence. You could mix all these variables into one bowl, and the result will be virtually identical! Indicators are mathematical models that appear complex to anyone. However, by combining several indicators and controlling the cycle of a stock, you stack the odds in your favor in order to obtain a better return on your transactions.

Legend

Here are the symbols used throughout this book to identify different types of signals appearing on technical analysis charts.

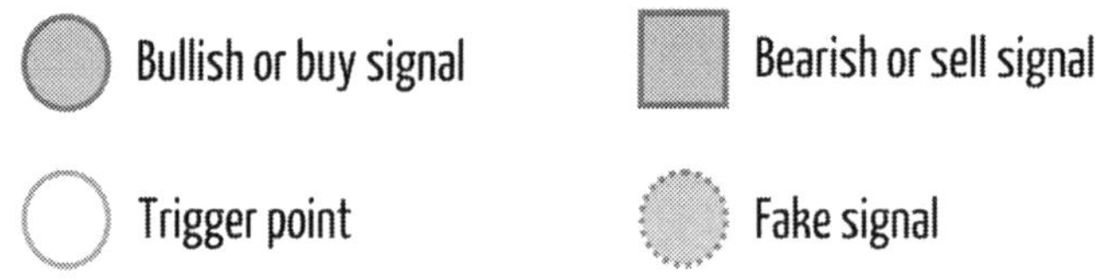

Now, it's time to start!

Chapter 1 – What is Technical Analysis?

Technical analysis is nothing more than the graphic representation of a financial stock, which highlights its strengths and weaknesses by using various indicators. Some websites even allow adding lines, drawings, and comments in order to make a better presentation of a stock's trend and its support and resistance zone. Be aware: indicators do not foretell the future. They can help anticipate it through some patterns. After gaining experience, you will know how to anticipate certain actions of the market.

You must also learn to read the information contained in a stock chart. A stock chart is the graphic representation of a stock price in a time frame divided into different types of periods: minutes, hours, days, weeks, months, quarters, etc. A stock chart presents a lot of information about price fluctuation as well as the trading volume. Furthermore, it's also possible to add a lot of indicators, each one as distinct as the other. Here is a list of free stock chart providers:

- Barchart
- Big Charts.com
- Free Stock Charts
- Google Finance
- StockCharts
- Stockopedia
- Stock Technical Analysis
- Trading View
- Yahoo! Finance

Before investing in a stock, it's vital to understand the information contained in a chart in order to be able to make the best investment decisions. It's similar to what you do when it's time to buy a computer or a smartphone. You examine the technical features, and you make comparisons between the different products in order to make the best decision.

Type of Charts

There are several ways of representing stock prices. We can use the Open-High-Low-Close (OHLC) chart, the candlestick chart, the line chart, the dot, the area and many others. Here are three usual ways of showing the evolution of a stock price in a short period of time.

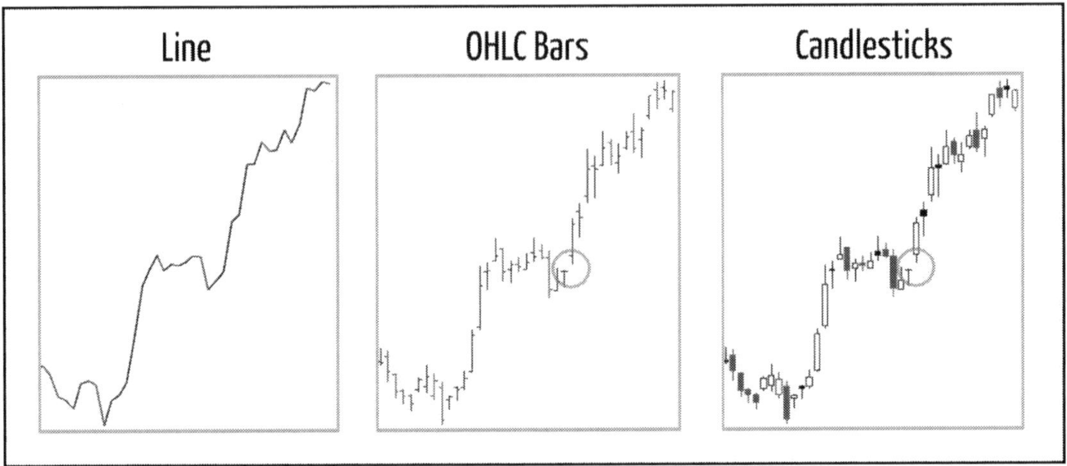

Figure 1.1: Type of charts

The first chart format is a simple line. The only information found on this basic chart is the closing price for each time unit. Charted together, a large number of units takes the shape of a curve; this is most often used for a long-term chart. The second format is the Open-High-Low-Close (OHLC) bars. It's a bar chart used to illustrate the movements of a financial stock in time. Each vertical line on the chart represents a time unit, for example, a week, a day or an hour. Each time unit is represented by an up-and-down shaft and two small horizontal traits. The one to the left corresponds to the price at the opening of the markets. The one to the right shows the price at the close of the markets.

The third format, the Japanese candlestick chart, presents the same information as the OHLC graph, but it has other advantages. Reading is simpler and faster. Note the similarity between the OHLC and the candlesticks. The trigger point displays a space between two bars and two candlesticks. This space is called a GAP and is often seen as a sign that announces a beautiful increase. This information is essential for the investor and is missing from the first format.

Candlesticks in Detail

The Japanese candlestick chart has been used for hundreds of years by Japanese retailers. This style of drawing the exchange rate of rice in one day has been simply applied to better interpret the price of a stock. It's pleasant-looking and shows all the information required to analyze each trading day. The only fault we could find is that its representation allows displaying smaller periods of time compared to others. The width of a candlestick is greater than the OHLC bar. For the purposes of this book, we will focus on the Japanese candlesticks that provide the most complete information and which are by far the best expression of a stock chart.

Figure 1.2 illustrates in detail a positive and a negative day on the stock market. According to the platforms we've used, a positive day will be symbolized by a white or green candlestick, and a negative day will be represented by a red or black candlestick.

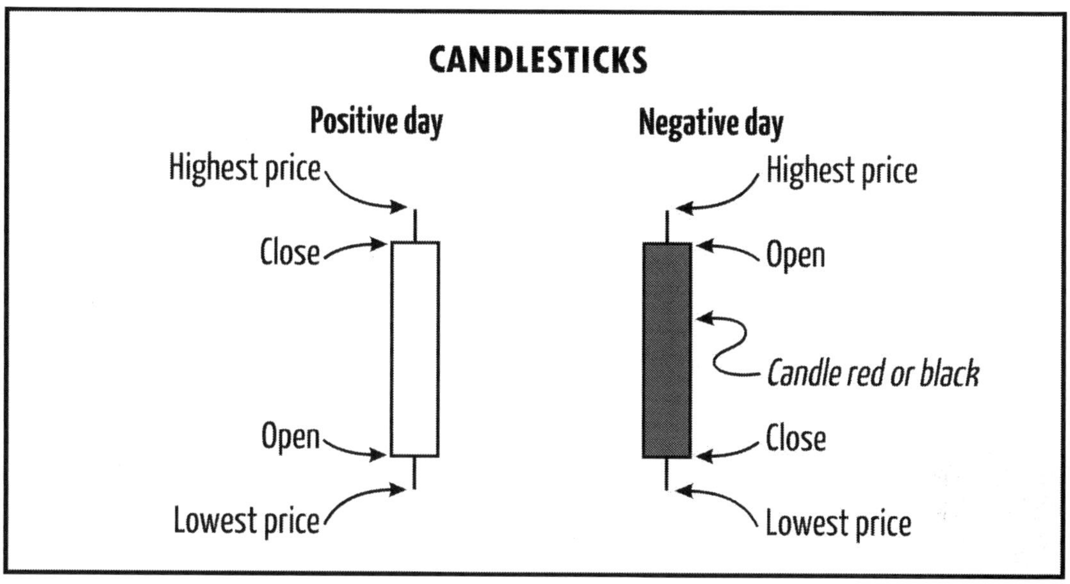

Figure 1.2: Japanese candlesticks

The rectangular bodies show the interval between the opening and the closing of a transaction period. The two fine black traits, called shadows, show extreme levels of the day. These traits are missing when the opening and closing of the stock is made at one of its extremes. The candlestick's length shows the strength that separates the lowest and the highest price. When the candlesticks for some days are shorter, there is a common ground between the bulls and the bears.

When the closing level is getting closer to the highest price of the day, this indicates that the buyers have taken control. A positive beginning can be foreseen for the next morning. When the closing level is getting closer to the lowest price of the day, this indicates that the sellers are getting rid of their stocks. A negative start can be foreseen for the next morning. We can count around a hundred candlestick setups which offer clues about the future direction of stock price. A few patterns are presented in *Chapter 11*. Many works have been written in this field. Feel free to read them to perfect your knowledge.

Chapter 2 – Preliminary Analysis

This chapter presents some elements to consider in order to properly plan the purchase of securities. Taking the time to invest in a stock does not only mean waiting for the ideal technical moment; other precautions are considered necessary before investing in a stock. Too many novices dive into a stock without taking the time to do some research about the targeted company.

Despite an extremely bullish chart, your stock could be on the way to presenting disastrous quarterly results. How do you prevent such a situation? Simply don't invest ahead of the announcement of the financial results! Take care of making your duties consciously in order to avoid falling into the many traps set by the pros.

1. Analyze the market and make sure the trend is positive.

- Check the market trend.
- Check the sector trend.
- Buy stock in a rising market.

2. Validate the recommendations made by your guru.

- Consider that the guru is ready to liquidate positions into strength even before you are invested.
- Consider only the selections made by the gurus whose securities are well supported by well-documented graphics.
- Do not chase any recommended stock that has won big percentage points in previous days.
- Avoid the traps from the discussion forums.
- Avoid the traps set by the 'pump-and-dump' websites.

3. Study the company you want to invest in and the one that has been recommended to you.

- What is the profile of the company, what is its history? What is its integrity level? What are the main competitors?
- What is the date for the next financial results? Unless you are a soothsayer, never keep or buy a stock before the announcement of the quarterly results.
- What is the latest news concerning the company?

4. Strict trading rules to follow.

In order to avoid falling into the traps that the market makers could set, be careful and get ready for anything that may come your way.

- Before buying, establish your selling target. Limit your objectives for gaining.
- Never invest more than $2,000–$2,500 in one stock.
- Never invest in small companies rated as 'pink sheet.'
- Never chase the stock you want to have at all costs.
- Never hold more than three stocks at the same time.
- Never invest 100% of your assets.
- Never focus your acquisitions in the same sector.
- Never increase a losing position.
- Never invest in a stock without a clearly defined trend and not supported by a good volume.
- Never invest in a stock that has registered a massive decline after an amazing increase. The final rebound is impossible to forecast.
- Never fall in the day-trading trap—you will be ruined!
- Never hesitate to sell a losing position.
- Never invest in the first 10–15 minutes after the market's opening. The stocks often make a pullback between 10:00 and 10:30.
- Never invest in stocks whose average daily volume for 30 days is less than 100,000 shares.

5. Trading psychology.

You have probably seen one of your friends losing control of his emotions before. Prepare yourself because the trading world can make you go through all the existing emotions. Key points to remember:

- Never blindly trust your friends and gurus. Do your own research before trading.
- Remain modest; the market will remind you of this quickly.
- Remain calm and put your emotions aside.
- Never fall in love with a stock.
- Don't believe that you will make a profit in each of your transactions. Your success does not depend on the quality of your technical analysis. Rather, it depends on your capacity to manage your emotions.
- Take your profit when you can—you will not have a second chance.

Chapter 3 – The Trend

A key element in the technical analysis is to determine in which stage a stock is located. This step is essential. It's very reassuring to know you have just invested in a stock that is going through a favorable period. Stage identification allows you to establish whether the stock is bullish, bearish or in a consolidation period.

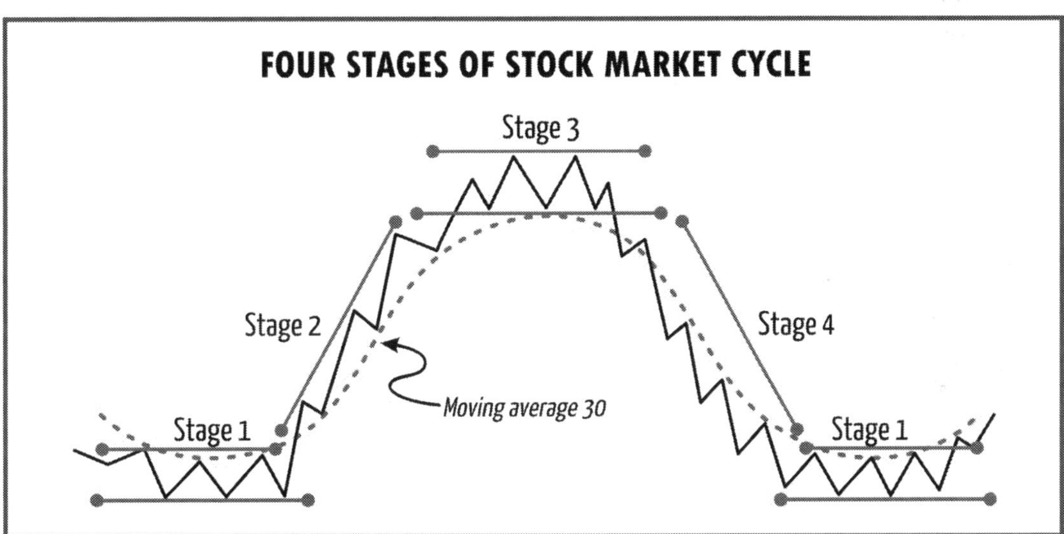

Figure 3.1: Four stages of the stock market cycle

Look at these stages as the four seasons when the temperature levels swing back and forth from day to day to form a cycle. The temperature goes up in the spring, becomes steady at a high level in the summer, decreases in the autumn and becomes stable at a low level in the winter. Here are the stages to consider.

Stage 1

The foundation or consolidation stage: Purchases and sales are balanced. The volume decreases. The market is reasonably stable. The moving average flattens. The stock price is facing resistance. At the end of this first stage, the volumes should increase, and the prices should position on the moving average.

Stage 2

The breakout stage: The best moment to buy occurs when price crosses above the 30-period moving average (SMA30). The ascent stage 1 occurs on rising volumes. The beginning of stage 2 is seen as a series of price increases, which could be jerky, with no significant lows and fixed by stronger volumes. The demand is supported by buyers, who do not want to miss the rally.

Stage 3

The ceiling stage: The share price enters into a rebalancing period. The latecomers buy, and the pros sell their shares. We get back to a balance between the selling and the buying-related price. It's an irregular market where new highs can be reached. Volume is lower. The SMA30 flattens and falls below the stock price.

Stage 4

The breakdown stage: The sellers take the lead. The prices are below the SMA30, which begins to bend. The share price tends to decline quickly during the break. Regularly, we see an increase in the volume. It can be a slow agony or a severe drop. Your investment strategy has to be different from one stage to the other. It can be difficult to detect the beginning and the end of the stages. This is why you should use a SMA30 or an exponential moving average of 34 periods (EMA34). When the stock price crosses one of these averages, it should be considered a stage change.

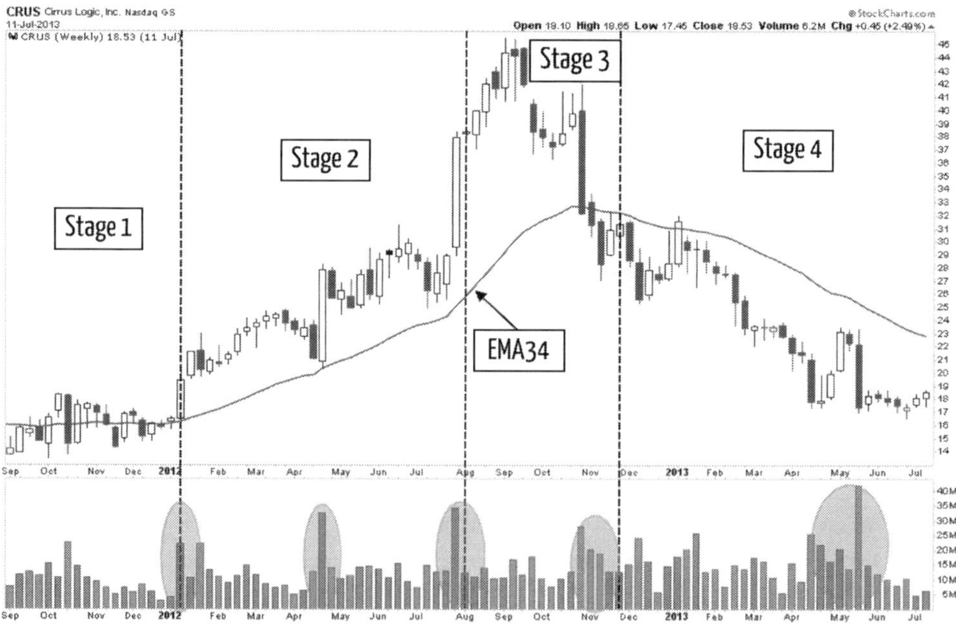

Figure 3.2: Cirrus Logic and stages

Figure above shows the four stages in a weekly format for Cirrus Logic, which staggers for a three-year period. It's always recommended you identify the stages by using a weekly chart. Daily charts offer too much volatility, which makes it more difficult to identify stages properly. Normally, the purchase of a share should be made at the beginning of stage 2, and the sale should be made at the beginning of stage 4.

A Simple Tool

The trend concept is relatively simple. The trend defines the direction of stocks or markets. The trend may be positive or negative. A market may go up or go down, and it happens frequently to see a market without any trend, as if it were at a standstill. This type of market occurs when buyers and sellers agree on a price. You should always invest in the trend's direction. You should never go against the wave and try to guess the trend reversals. The market will take you back on the right way quickly. A stock with a confirmed positive trend will produce significant profits. Always sell when a trend reversal occurs.

The Trend Line

The trend line is the most underestimated element in technical analysis. However, the simple fact of showing the direction and the momentum of a stock can be enough to establish our investment strategy. The direction can result in the increase or the decrease of the share's price. The momentum can be translated as the strength of the inclination of this trend. The trend line is an extremely uncommon tool on which you have full control. Among other things, it allows you to predict the trend reversals likely to occur, either positive or negative. No mathematical formula is required.

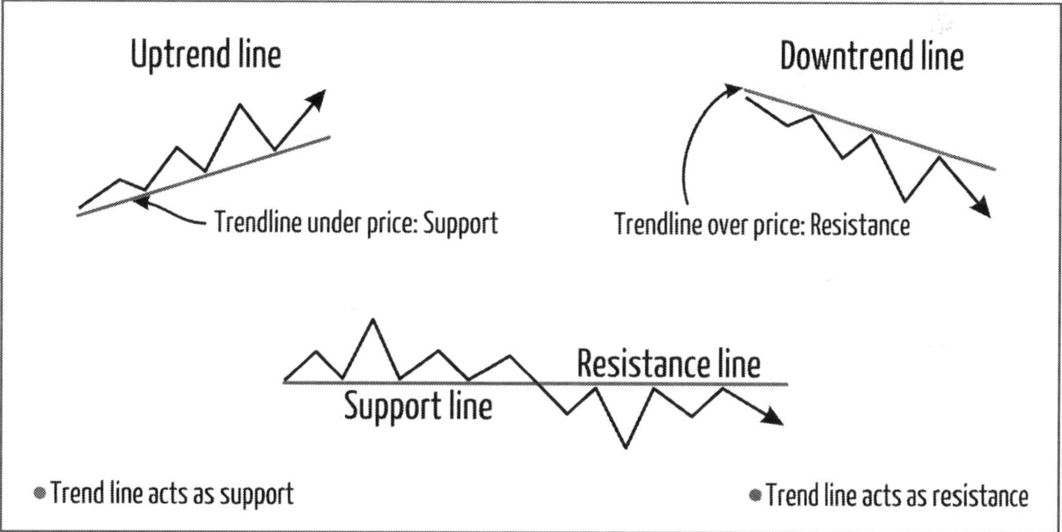

Figure 3.3: Trend lines

We can consider three types of trend lines: the uptrend line with a positive slope, the downtrend line with a negative slope, and the trend line with no slope, which is, in fact, a support or a resistance line. To be valid, the trend line has to be drawn so that it touches at least three candlesticks. The higher the number of candlesticks, the more significant is the trend line. When the trend is upward, the trend line has to be drawn so that it connects the base between the candlesticks. When the trend is downward, the trend line has to be drawn so that it connects the top between the candlesticks. The breaking of a trend line does not mean that a new trend has begun. It can be a false signal.

Uptrend Line

The uptrend line is helpful because it provides an upcoming indication of a downward exit point. This line looks like an increase. Some of them are abrupt, while others are scarcely tilted. The uptrend line represents a form of support with an upward trend. To be valid, the uptrend line has to be touched at least three times by one of the candlesticks, and it has to be drawn below the candlesticks. The break of this trend line sends the signal of a possible trend reversal. It's time to think about selling your stocks if your investment horizon is short-term.

Figure 3.4: Dow Jones and uptrend lines

The Dow Jones shows four positive trends as well as four reversals. When a breakdown appears, an increase in volume is not required. However, the increase in volume may be felt if the stock loses value quickly and panic sets in on the market. The abrupt slope of a trend line would have more probabilities of breaking fast because the support doesn't have the time to be put in place.

Downtrend Line

The downtrend line provides indications of an upward exit point. The strength of this decline may fluctuate: some of them are steep, others are barely tilted. The downtrend line is a kind of resistance with a downward trend. To valid a downtrend line, the candlesticks must touch it at least three times. After gaining some experience, you will notice that all the investors become agitated at the same time when a breakout or a breakdown occurs. You are not the only one who has foreseen the breaking zone of a stock.

Many other traders have noticed it. You have to act fast in order to maximize the opportunity that is being offered to you. The volume must be upward so that the break becomes relevant. To be valid, the breakout of a downtrend line must be made completely through volumes that are three to five times the average volume of the last 30 periods. The rising break represents a buy signal. From this point forward, buyers assume control of the marketplace.

Figure 3.5: Canadian Solar and downtrend line

Canadian Solar has been dealing with a succession of downtrends, as the solar market has been losing its power of attraction since March 2014. Pay attention to three breaking points; each represents an excellent opportunity to purchase the stock.

Support and Resistance

Support and resistance are quite easy to master; these features must be part of your toolbox. Above all, don't underestimate the importance of the support and resistance, which are essential to master technical analysis concepts. They symbolize the marking levels that buyers and sellers recognize and that make them act in consensus. Figure 3.6 shows a graphic representation of a stock whose price runs into resistance and support. Make use of discipline by drawing lines of support and resistance, and you'll come out a winner. By mastering these levels, you can predict future rebounds.

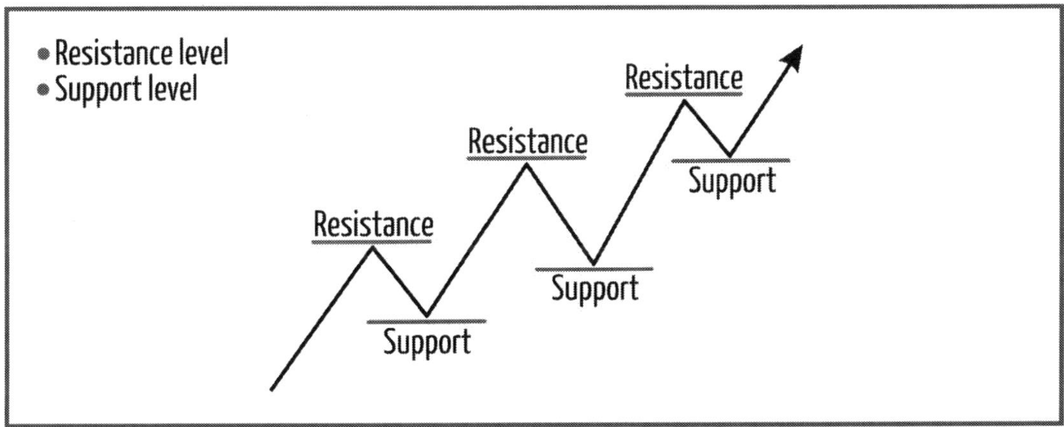

Figure 3.6: Support and resistance

The support is a zone that the buyers find attractive. In this zone, the buyers dominate and push the market up. On the other hand, the resistance is a zone where the sellers have control, and therefore, they pull the market down. The support shows the lowest level where the share price could bounce. Demand is firmer than supply, which prevents the stock from collapsing below the support. The more the support zone is tested, the stronger it will become. The longer the support period, the stronger it will become.

However, the time wears out, and the support will eventually decline. Some investors will give up, and they will be replaced by brand-new investors who won't work with the same markers as the previous ones. The resistance and support stages evolve over time, according to the new reality of the financial markets. There is a tendency to draw the support with one line only, and it's good to do it like that. Nevertheless, a support should have a certain thickness. The wider the candlesticks' range as a support zone, the greater the margin of error in evaluating possible rebounds will be.

To make a better evaluation of the support zone, take the time to analyze the stock in a weekly mode. The zone might be different, and you might reach the conclusion that changing the entry and exit targets is required. The support evolves according to the stock price. Volume fluctuations also lead to a variation in the stock price at different levels of trade. Figure 3.7 shows that Netflix has bounced back five times on the support zone within a year. If the downward break of the support happens, the stock can continue to decrease as long as brand-new support and fresh buyers are missing.

Figure 3.7: Netflix and support zone

The resistance refers to the level that stock price could hit during the surge of a stock price. The sellers do not believe in a higher level and cash in their profits when the stock price touches the resistance. These are two opposing strategies. While the crowd believes in a breakout, the pros sell when the stock price faces the resistance. The demand is simply not strong enough to cause an upward break. The pros take advantage to do a short sale and pocket the losses of the buyers who believed they are buying at the right time.

Like the support zone, the longer the resistance zone is, the stronger it will become. Additionally, use the weekly chart to validate the long-term resistance. The more the resistance is tested, the stronger it will become. This means that many investors have extrapolated a break which was late and which brought in other investors to give it a chance. The more the resistance is tested, the more likely it is the break will cause a significant rise.

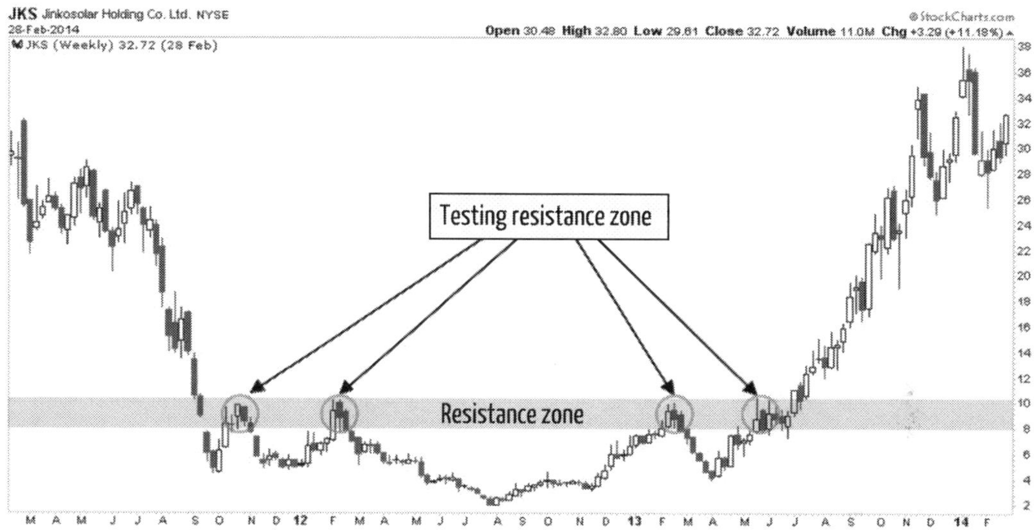

Figure 3.8: Jinkosolar Holding and resistance zone

Jinkosolar Holding suffered an outstanding drop from July to October 2011. Since then, the stock has touched its resistance of $10 several times, which led to a major resistance. When this resistance zone is clear, it will turn into a support zone. Support and resistance zones evolve over time. A resistance strength with a limit of $3.00 for a stock will not be the same next month. The market evolves day by day, with old investors giving way to new ones.

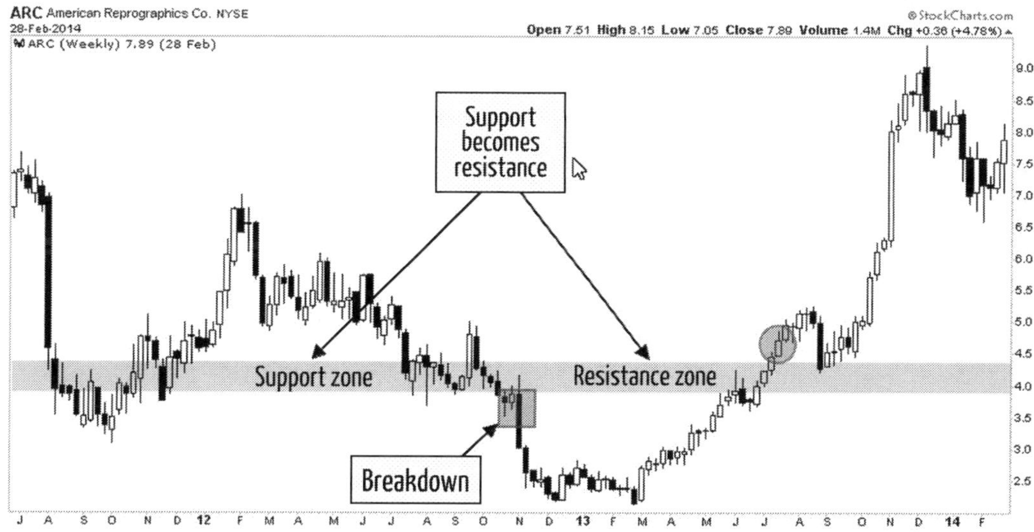

Figure 3.9: American Reprographics, support and resistance

The figure 3.9 shows American Reprographics and a support zone which turns into a resistance zone. Support at $4.00 has been tested several times. It also broke during the mini-crash of October 2011. The stock price has come back to test the support zone in August 2011, to break through in September and October 2011. The stock price stumbled again on this support from July to September 2012. In early November 2012, the support zone collapsed, and the stock lost half of its value in less than two months. The stock moves to a fresh new low, and support zone has transformed into a resistance.

> **TACTICS – Support and resistance**. The resistance is the level where the stock could stumble over during the increase of the share price. The support refers to the level on which the stock price rebounds during the decline of the share price.

Trend Channel

The trend channel draws its origin from the trend line, to which is added a parallel line to form a corridor. A trend channel looks like a rectangle in which the stock price bounces back many times between its upper and lower limits.

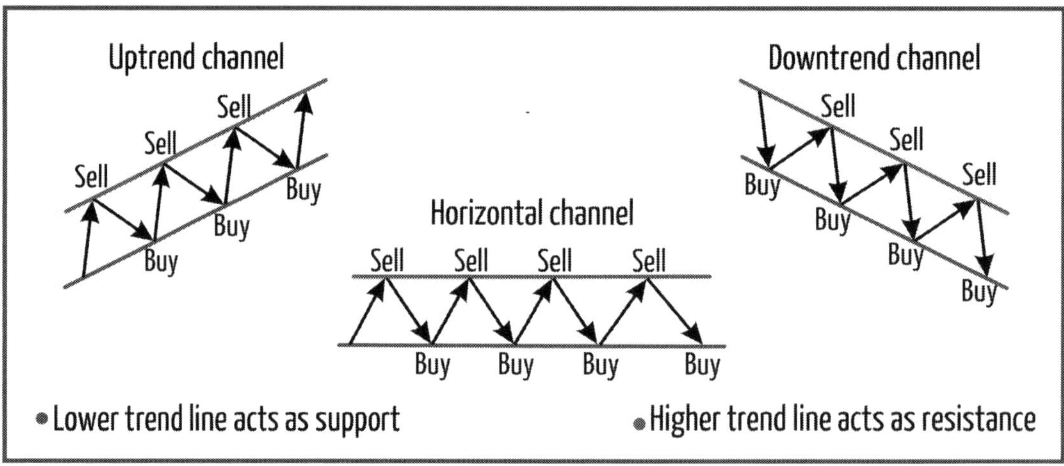

Figure 3.10: Channel. As the trend lines, we count three trend channels or corridors: an uptrend channel with a positive slope, a downward channel with a negative slope, and a trend channel without any slope.

The top red line represents the resistance, and the lower green line represents the support. The way of treating the rebounds on resistance and on support is identical to one of the trend lines. The stock price stumbles over the resistance line and remains within the trend channel. The same happens with the support line: the stock price stumbles over the support line and remains within the trend channel.

> **TACTICS – Trend line and trading range**. A trend line is a straight line which, to be meaningful, must touch the base or the top of candlesticks at least three times. The use of the trend line or channel allows anticipating the buy and sell levels. The longer the line is, the stronger the breakout will become.

Divergence

Divergence can be defined as a difference, an opposition, or a contradiction between two elements. The concept of divergence remains quite simple, but many people have difficulty mastering it. Using indicators often highlights the divergence between the stock price and indicators. There are divergences or contradictions because the indicator does not move in the same way as the stock price. There are two types of divergences: the upward or positive divergence and the downward or negative divergence. An upward divergence occurs when the indicator is up, and the stock price is down. Usually, it's followed by an interesting boost in the share price.

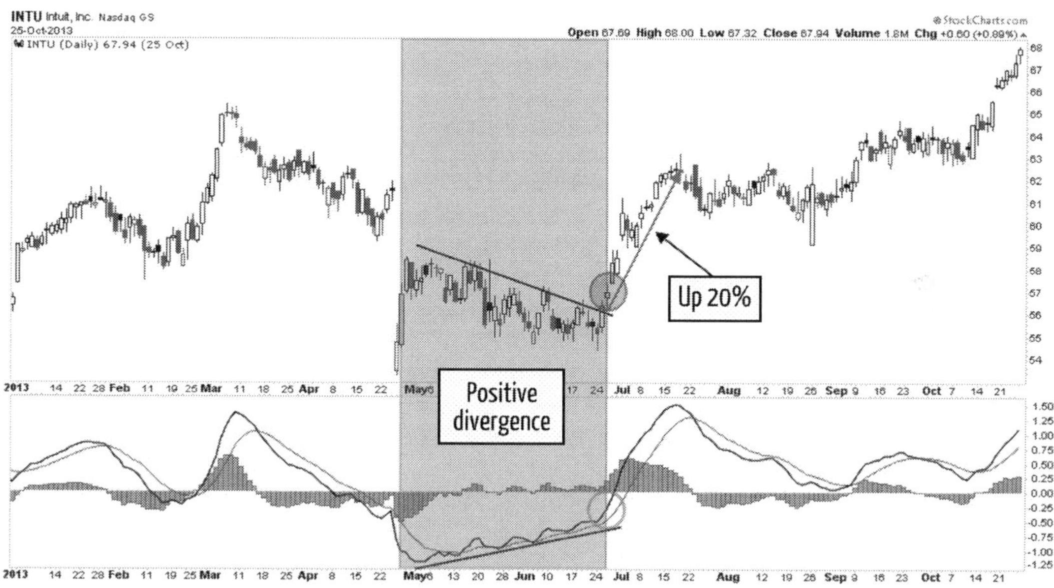

Figure 3.11: Intuit and positive divergence

The MACD indicator was added to the chart of Intuit Company. The gray area represents the divergence zone. The MACD is up, while the stock price is down. At the end of this zone, the stock price makes a steep increase and gains almost 20% in less than a month. The positive divergence allows the investor to see the potential increase, which is about to start.

Put aside the stocks that present upward divergences and take action when the stock passes above the downtrend line. Conversely, a downward divergence occurs when the indicator is down, and the stock price reaches a new high. It's quite possible that a dip in the stock price might appear, but this doesn't occur automatically. It can give a false signal. In case of doubt, restrain yourself and pass to another stock.

Figure 3.12: Lululemon and negative divergence

The weekly graph of Lululemon Athletica shows a perfect bearish divergence. The MACD indicator is declining while the share price continues to grow and finally falls more than 27%. The negative divergence allows the investor to anticipate the possible decrease which is about to be triggered. Put aside the stocks with downward divergences. If you are looking for a long-term investment, wait for an upward reversal before buying.

Chapter 4 – Recognizing Breakout

In the previous chapter, we discovered the importance of tracing the trend lines and channels. The most important element brought by drawing these lines is the ability to provide landmarks in the projection of a future upward or downward break. The trend line break signals that the trend has just changed direction. Take action by selling your shares or by purchasing the coveted stock.

Breakout

Technically speaking, a breakout occurs when there is a break of a resistance. This break has to be accompanied by a significant volume increase that must be three to five times the average volume of the last 30 days. Many small investors base their trading strategy on the break of a major resistance. The figure below shows the basic patterns of a breakout. It can occur during a positive trend, during a consolidation period or during a downward trend. Often, the stock takes a pause after the breakout and then tests the support zone before continuing its increase. This scenario is represented by the dotted lines.

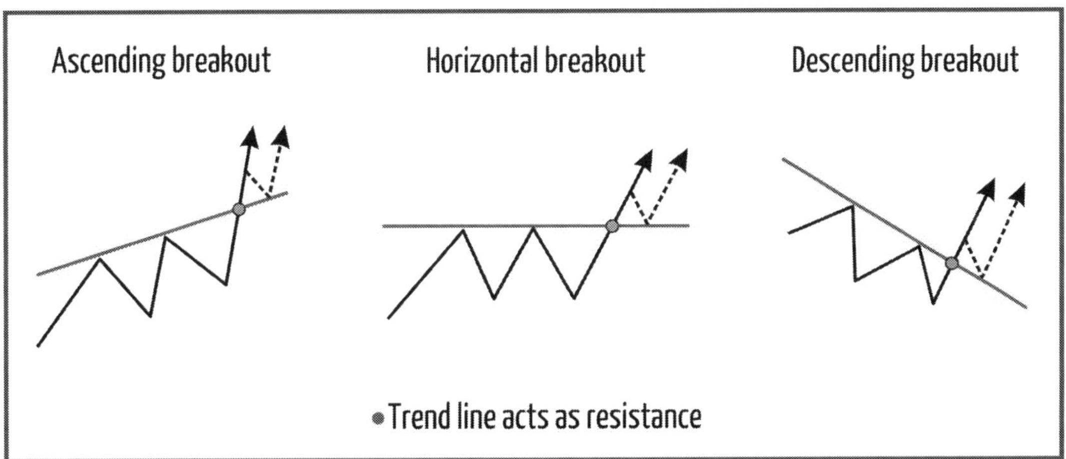

Figure 4.1: Upside breakout

This strategy remains one of the most famous. However, you should consider that an important number of signals remains invalid. In fact, professionals have understood that many investors target these levels and take advantage to sell when the breakout is about to occur, so you end up getting a fake signal. A true breakout needs some specifications to be valid. Foremost of all, there is a fairly long consolidation period preceding the breakout. Why? We have to give the stock time to build a good resistance, which, once surpassed, will become a strong support. Let's take the example of a breakout that happens after a period of consolidation of five days. It's likely that the stock should return below the resistance because the support generated like that would be too weak to contain the future sellers who may want to get rid of the stock.

Second, the resistance needs to be tested a few times in order to be recognized. The more the stock stumbles over a resistance, the stronger it becomes. Identify the stocks that have a consolidation of 30–40 periods. The base will be solid, and the stock's explosion will be much more vigorous. Third, the most important element concerns the volume and it validates the upward break of the trend.

Figure 4.2: L&L Energy and a Breakout

Pay attention to the volume level following the upside breakout of L&L Energy in early April 2013. Rising volume propelled the stock from \$2 to \$5 in less than three weeks. This volume increase is more than three to five times higher than the average of the last 30 periods, represented by the blue line in the volume window. The accumulation period between May 2012 and April 2013 allows creating significant gain.

Figure 4.3: TransEnterix and a breakout

Consider the upside breakout for TransEnterix at the beginning of August. The stock more than doubled in a single session. Do you miss that breakout? There's no need to worry. The stock comes back to test its support zone four days later, before pursuing its crazy ride. This pattern following a resistance breakout frequently occurs. Never chase a stock. Place that stock on your watchlist. Wait two to three days to see whether it's testing the support zone again. Keep in mind that a stock will always make a downward correction, no matter the strength of the upward break. If not, pass to the next one. There are opportunities every day.

Breakdown

In contrast to the breakout, the breakdown occurs when there is a downward break of the support zone. The breakdown is caused when many investors have lost confidence in their stock for various reasons. This loss of confidence may be caused by a poor trend in the sector, bad economic news or other information that might impact the stock. Some congestion occurs before the break, similar to when workers hit a wall with a mass in order to break it. Because of the pressure applied at the same location, the wall will ultimately crumble.

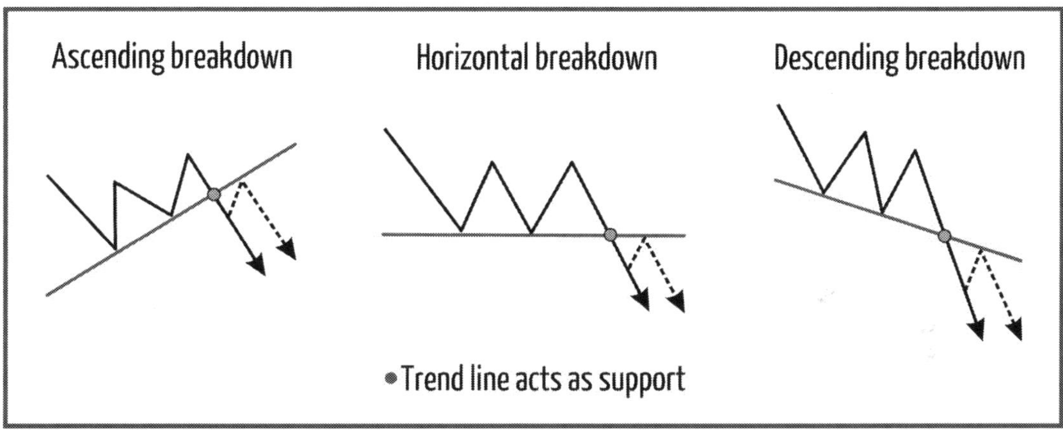

Figure 4.4: Breakdown

The figure above illustrates the basic form of a breakdown. It can happen during a positive trend, a consolidation period or a downward trend. Unlike the breakout, the breakdown does not need a volume increase in order to be valid. A volume increase directly leads to a faster decline of the stock. The downward break of a strong support zone leads to a significant drop in the share. The breakdown is characterized by a total disinterest in a stock. It follows numerous attempts to break support. The strength of the support is proportional to the number of bounces.

Look at the figure 4.5 of Barrick Gold. Between November 2014 and July 2015, there were numerous rebounds in the support zone. The buyers trusted in an upward return, and this happened three times. Consequently, the support zone has been tested again and collapsed in July 2015. Notice the volume increase during the downward break. Shareholders abandoned the stock massively, creating panic. As mentioned earlier, the volume increase is not required during a breakdown. If there is one, the disruption will be even more efficient.

Figure 4.5: Barrick Gold and a breakdown

Channel Break

As we saw earlier, the trend channel is made of two parallel lines within which the stock price bounces back many times. The channel can be bullish, bearish or without any slope. We must realize that a stock in a positive trend channel can break upward of the upper line of the channel, or it can go under the lower line of the channel. Securities and mutual funds move as bullish or bearish cycles. Look at the breaks that occur in the opposite direction of the trend channel.

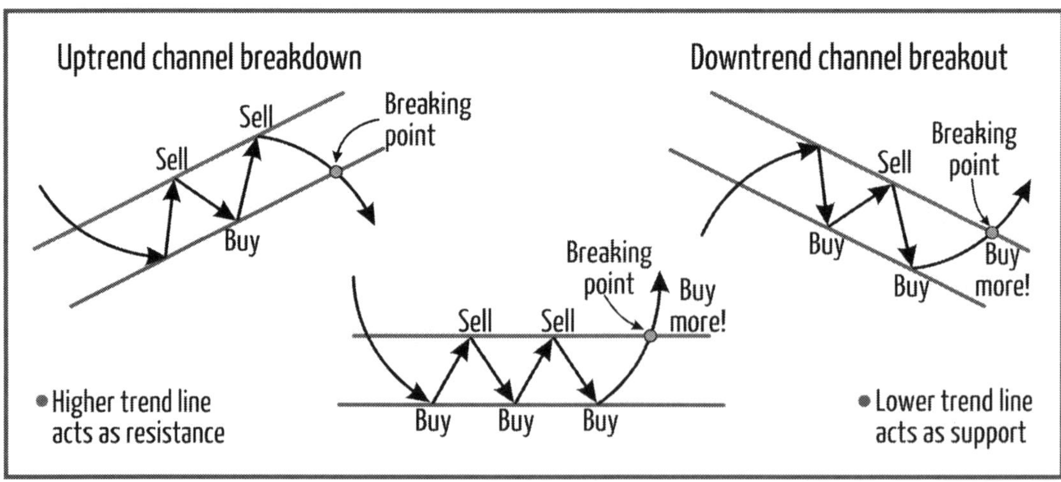

Figure 4.6: How to Trade a channel breakout

The figure above demonstrates how to play the break of an upward trend channel, a downward trend channel, and in a flat trading range. These models allow investors to anticipate a break with a significant impulse of the stock price. Get used to drawing your lines and trend channel, and your performance will register a solid increase.

Short Selling

In contrast to the market in general (being long or long position), many professionals use the trading strategy of short-selling the securities that are experiencing the breakdown. Without elaborating further measures, short-selling involves selling a stock that you do not possess, which will be bought at a cheaper price. This is the opposite of those who buy cheap and hope to sell at a higher price.

The concept may be confusing, but it's still quite simple. Your brokerage firm lends you a stock you agree to repurchase for a lower price. Several traders are masters in the use of this strategy. They must continually be glued to their screens to raise gains successfully. They primarily attack stocks that have increased excessively and which, sooner or later, will break from the pressure.

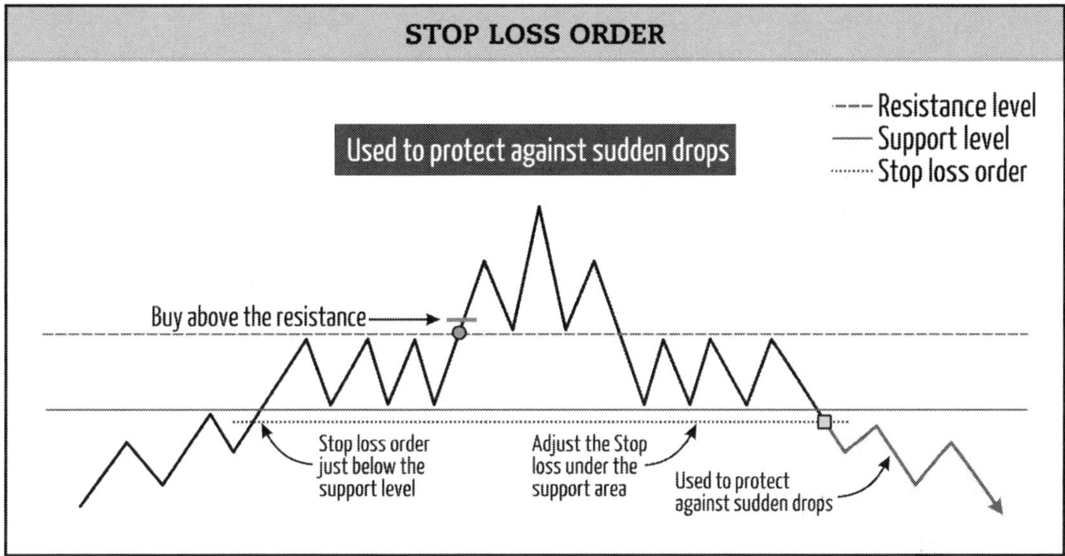

Figure 4.7: A stop loss order

A stop order is not recommended for stocks with average volume of fewer than 100,000 units. These stocks have a big trading range, which guarantees the triggering of stop orders. If you lose 10 percent in each of your transactions, there is a great risk of destroying your chances of success. Learn how to manage risk, and protect your capital above all else.

Chapter 5 – Trend Indicators

Various indicators remain at our disposal to analyze the chart of a stock. The indicators are primarily mathematical models based on two variables: stock price and periods. Each indicator has its strength. Use indicators as a complement to support, resistance and trend line. Let's start with the group of indicators used to follow trends: Simple Moving Average (SMA), Exponential Moving Average (EMA), Moving Average Convergence Divergence (MACD), Average Directional Index (ADX), Parabolic SAR and Force index.

The trend indicators, as suggested by their names, allow you to highlight the trend of the market and stocks. The trend indicators are useful in sustaining the momentum indicators that we will see in Chapter 6. They have the advantage of giving a proven indication of the trend and the strength of this trend. The trends evolve cyclically, following an up-and-down sequence. Trend indicators do not predict the future. No indicator can predict the future with accuracy. Still, it is reassuring to rely on such indicators when it is time to invest or sell. Furthermore, these indicators add weight to the trend line you have drawn. The combination of several indicators will be more than positive and should improve your decisions before buying, selling or keeping a stock you already own.

Simple Moving Average (SMA)

The simple moving average represents the average price of a share over a given period. It's called moving because it moves from one period to another. Figure 5.1 presents, through trigger points, the moving average for the last 20 days. The gray zones form two independent groups of 20 days (from July 12 to August 8 and September 19 to October 17). A new 20-day period moving average is calculated under the candlesticks chart.

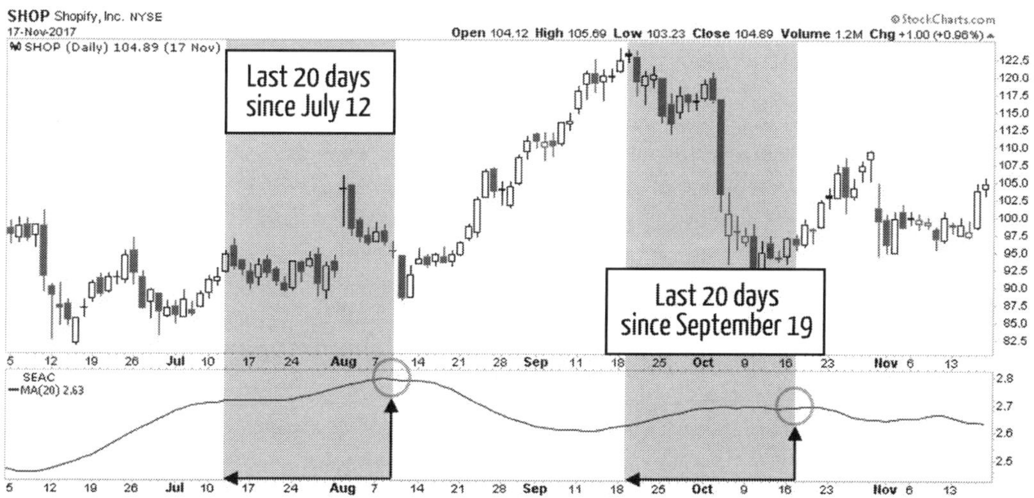

Figure 5.1: Shopify and SMA20

The SMA is calculated starting from the number of periods (minutes, hours, days, weeks, weeks or months) listed in the settings of your provider. The calculation is very simple: it adds the closing price of the last 20 days, then divides by 20. To calculate the average of the following day, just remove the old date and add the most recent day. The juxtaposition of each day's average generates a smooth curve. The SMA also allows viewing the trend of the stock and identifying the change of the trend.

The shorter the moving average is, the more the moving average sticks to the trend. The more you increase the number of periods of the moving average, the more the gap between the average and the stock price will increase. The most popular averages are of 9, 13, 20, 30, 40, 50, 100, 150 and 200 periods. The crowd typically sticks with averages of 50 and 200 periods. Use an average that connects the best with your trading style. If you invest short-term, use the 30-day or 50-day moving average; if you invest long-term, use the 150-day or 200-day moving average.

Figure 5.2: Yahoo and SMA

It may seem that the price of a share tends to bounce on a moving average. It's not quite so. In fact, many investors check the same moving average, which makes the stock react at the same time. No matter the moving average used, you should buy a stock only when the slope of the moving average is rising. The rise of Yahoo stock, during the first six months of 2013, was absolutely amazing. Strangely, the SMA30 looks like a trend line.

The moving average, like all indicators, has a very nasty fault: It is a delayed indicator. It is late compared to the stock price. The moving average is not up to date; it is disconnected from the reality of the day. In a market that moves fast, the use of the moving average will be inefficient, unless you have your eyes continuously connected to your screen. In the above chart, there's a lot of distortion around the trigger point. Be prepared to sell. It should be useful to add another indicator to confirm this bad signal.

If you glue a short period to a moving average, such as five-day moving average, it will follow the rhythm of the share very tightly. Short moving averages are used by day traders. They use the crossing of the moving average and the share price as a point of entry or exit. A high moving average, such as a 200-day moving average, will be less sensitive to the variations of the stock price. It is recommended for long-term investors who do not worry much about short-term fluctuations.

Figure 5.3: Kandi Technologies and SMA200 lagging

The figure above shows the impact generated by the 100% increase of Kandi Technologies on its 200-day moving average. The stock doubles in less than one week but has a slight impact on its moving average. As its name indicates, it is an average of the last 200 days. The delay between the SMA200 that points to $4 in early June and the stock price at $8 forces you to reevaluate the use of such an average. For this reason, favor the use of two moving averages.

The Strategy of Crossing Moving Averages

The decision to buy or sell may be made by using the intersection of two moving averages. This method consists of the use of two different moving averages, one for the short term and the other for the long term. The crossing, generated through the use of these averages, is a buy or sell signal. It is suggested that you buy when the short-term moving average crosses above the longest average. It is also advised that you sell when the short-term moving average crosses below the longer average. Use a combination of 13–30 or 20–40 to generate a short-term signal. For a medium term, use a combination of 20–40 or 30–50, and for a long-term use a 50–200.

There are an infinite number of combinations. You can combine three moving averages as 13-21-34. Some people prove their originality and even use the Fibonacci sequence, which was introduced by Leonardo de Pise, surnamed Fibonacci.

He was a mathematician of Italian origin who lived in the thirteenth century. The Fibonacci sequence is seen as the fact that each number, starting from the third one, is the sum of the two preceding numbers. Here is the beginning of the Fibonacci sequence:

1, 1, 2, 3, 5, 8, 13, 21, 34, 55, 89, 144, 233, . . .

The idea of using some of these numbers is not so far-fetched. Pay attention to the Fibonacci sequence and see that the numbers 13, 21 and 34 are numbers that often reappear in the use of moving averages and other indicators. Feel free to create and test your combination! A combination can be efficient for one stock and inefficient for another one. In *Chapter 12*, we'll use another concept of Fibonacci.

In figure 5.4, an upward increase occurs in the second week of October 2012. The market will be positive for the next eight months. A big resistance is drawn at $32 after a few months (dotted horizontal line). The stock reaches a $35 limit in December 2012, makes a drop on the support zone and explodes at the beginning of 2013. While a stock unleashes a positive trend reversal, it is wise to tie the moving average to the subsequent return. The SMA13 serves as a support and trend line for the next months. A week closing below this average will send a sell signal.

Figure 5.4: Cree and SMA 13-30

The combination of moving averages is a simple way to get buy and sell signals, but it also brings false signals. Avoid the signals generated during a consolidation period. The volume tends to decline in a consolidation area because investors move to the sidelines. A lot of investors are waiting for a big move before entering the market.

Exponential Moving Average (EMA)

An exponential moving average gives more weight to the most recent price instead of allocating the same weight every day as the simple moving average does. The exponential moving average is more spirited and responds faster to market volatility. Use a combination between the EMA13-30 or EMA13-34 on a weekly basis and pinpoint the cross of the trend reversal. These combinations are popular among the chartists.

Figure 5.5: Cree and EMA13-34

Consider that EMA13-34 combination of figure 5.5 is as sinuous as the SMA13-30 combination of figure 5.4. You will have noticed that the buy signal appears late compared to the SMA13-30. Exponential Moving Average has the advantage (and disadvantage) of being quicker to respond to the last price fluctuations than a Simple Moving Average.

Figure 5.6: Cree and EMA13-SMA30

It is also possible to combine one EMA and one SMA to obtain both sides of the medal. For example, combine SMA13 and EMA34. Differences are more perceptible during ups and downs. During the period of consolidation, there is very little contrast.

> **TACTICS - Moving Averages.** A strategy based on crossing moving averages is much more efficient than using a single moving average. A bullish cross is generated when the shorter moving average crosses above the long moving average. This often coincides with the start of stage 2. Make sure you have a positive slope. A bearish cross is generated when the short moving average crosses below the longest average. The slope of the moving average should be negative.

Moving Average Convergence Divergence (MACD)

The MACD is a superb trend indicator. It is surely one of the most favorite indicators of many expert traders. This indicator is composed of three exponential moving averages (by default 12, 26, 9), and it is represented by two curves: one slow-the signal line (thin line) and one fast-the MACD line (thicker line). The crossing of the two curves gives a trading signal. The signal is bullish when the fast MACD (thicker line) passes above the signal line (thin line). The signal is bearish when the fast MACD (thicker line) passes below the signal line (thin line).

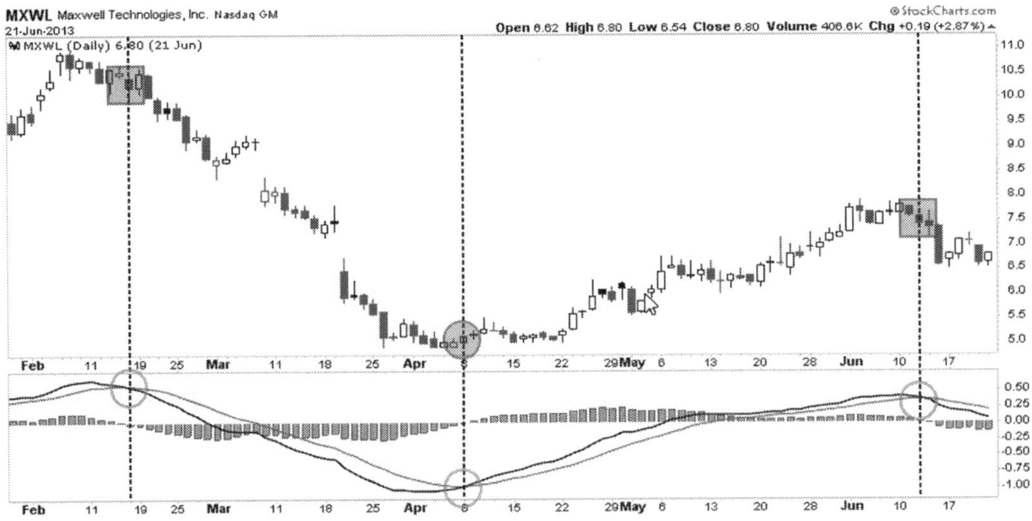

Figure 5.7: Maxwell Technologies and MACD

The above example shows the Maxwell Technologies stock with three superb MACD crossovers: one buy signal and two sell signals. MACD crossing indicates a change in the market trend. Notice how the signals have very little delay compared to the stock price. The farther the signal is away from zero, the more pertinent the signal will be. Furthermore, notice the beautiful amplitude of the indicator. These signals are reliable and indicate more precisely the direction the market will take. Favor stocks that offer this kind of amplitude—the suggested trend will be even more precise.

The MACD histogram is shown in the background as the vertical blue bars. The histogram represents the difference between the two curves of MACD and indicates a buy or sell signal when the MACD crossing is made. When the MACD indicator gives a buy signal, the histogram is above the zero line. The buyers took control. When the MACD indicator launches a sell signal, the histogram is below the zero line.

The slope of the histogram begins to turn upward March 27. This signal appeared five days before the signal from the MACD lines. Above all, don't forget the MACD histogram, as it is particularly efficient. The MACD indicator is also useful for detecting divergences. Remember that a divergence appears when the indicator goes against the stock price, and it allows identifying possible reversals. But these could be fake signals. Be careful using the divergences.

Apple shows, in the figure 5.8, a huge negative divergence beginning in March 2012. This divergence is extended to the six-month period. The MACD shows two buy signals and two sell signals. Following the first buy signal, the stock rallied from a low of $52 to a high of $80. During this period, the investors who took advantage of the rise still obtained a 50% gain in four months.

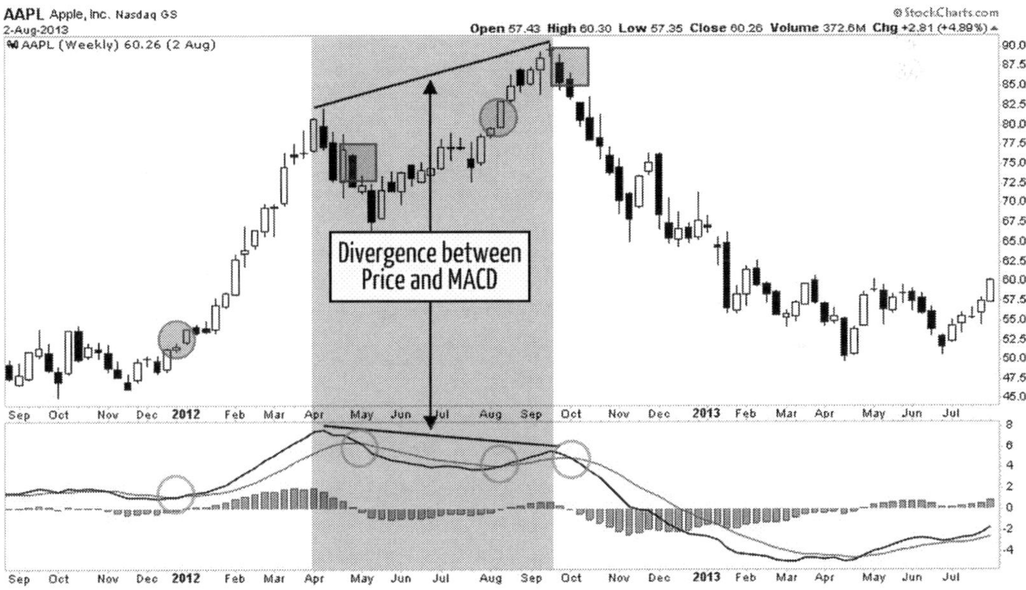

Figure 5.8: Apple and MACD divergence

Subsequently, the stock makes a pullback, and the MACD indicator starts a sell signal. However, the stock begins a second upward, and the MACD is launching a second buy signal. Buying when the MACD indicator shows a negative slope requires some temerity. The addition of other indicators would be desirable. Investors who bought from the first signal doubled their stake in less than nine months. The second sell signal is unambiguous; it's time to leave the ship. Investors should be more cautious when the MACD indicator crosses downward in October 2012.

Average Directional Index (ADX)

The average directional index (ADX) is a trend indicator as well as a trend strength indicator. This is a trading system on its own because it allows you to generate several signals. It is represented by three curves: +DI (green line), –DI (red line) and ADX (black line). The +DI measures the bullish pressure, while the –DI measures the bearish pressure. The ADX curve measures the force related to this upward or downward pressure. The ADX curve, used alone without the + Di and –Di indicators, should be considered as an indicator of volatility. It's important to remember that the ADX curve does not follow the trend of the market. It goes more in the direction of the market strength, upward as well as downward. This last concept is a little more difficult to understand.

It is common to go long when the +DI curve passes above the –DI curve. Your position will strengthen when the ADX indicator is in an uptrend. The +DI and –DI curves are the following trend indicators of this system. When the ADX is higher than 20–25, and the +DI curve passes above the –DI curve, a buy signal is generated. The ADX could be used on a daily or a weekly chart. When the ADX is higher than 20–25, and the –DI curve passes above the +DI curve, a sell signal is registered. It is crucial to consider not only the crossing of +DI and –DI as a buy signal. A buy signal is in place when a trend reversal of the +DI and –DI curves appears. Instead of waiting for the +DI to cross above the –DI, think about investing when the +DI comes out of a major low.

Let's take a look at figure 5.9 of Canadian Solar. See the time elapsed between the trigger point and the fake signal on the left. The yellow circles represent a trend reversal of the +DI indicator. This is a first positive sign before obtaining a buy signal. Notice that the first crossing between the +DI and –DI appeared late compared to the preceding trigger point. There is no expansion of the +Di; this is a fake signal. It takes too much time to send a buy signal.

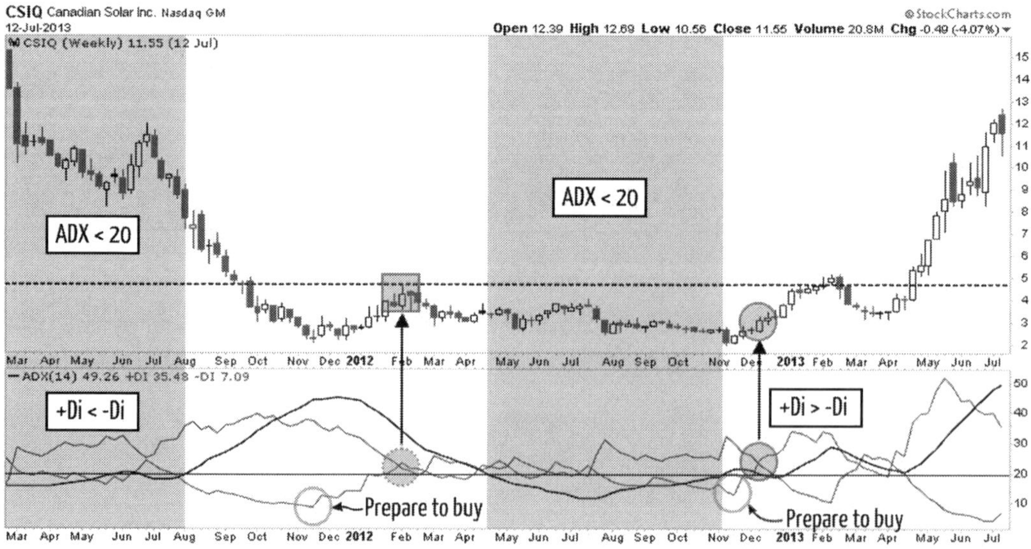

Figure 5.9: Canadian Solar and ADX

Strong buy signals appear when the ADX is placed significantly below the level 20, and the +DI crosses above the –DI as represented by the green circle. Complete this with a strong volume, and you'll have an exponential rise. The ADX measures the power of the trend. The higher it is, the stronger the trend. Pay attention to the first climb of the ADX that reaches level 45.

Just before, a strong downward movement was established, the Canadian Solar lost 80% of its value in five months. Investors sold out their shares massively, which led to a faster drop of the stock. On the other side, we can see the same phenomenon but opposite. At the beginning of 2013, the stock has grown from $3 to $12 in less than three months. The powerful rise was confirmed by a quick surge of the ADX.

> **TACTICS – ADX**. The positive trend is confirmed when the +DI crosses the -DI and ADX exceeds 20. Consider investing when the +DI begins to form a significant depression. The decline of the ADX signals the consolidation or the indecision of the market. Avoid transactions during this period. The ADX indicates the power of the trend. ADX may be high during a bullish or bearish market. When the ADX falls below 10, the stock is in a trading range.

Parabolic SAR

The Parabolic SAR, where SAR means 'stop and reversal,' is an indicator created by J. Welles Wilder. This indicator informs about potential trend changes in stock price or stock market index. It clearly shows the beginning and the end of a trend. Parabolic SAR is represented by small squares placed above or below the candlesticks. A square below the candlestick indicates that the trend is upward. A square above the candlestick indicates that the trend is downward. Pay attention to the trend changes; the square changes place. The signal is simple but useful.

The calculation for setting up the resultant curve of the parabolic SAR is complicated. We would rather explain its use. To understand better, pay attention to the chart of Advanced Micro Devices from figure 5.10. The small squares over and under the stock price represent the trend and are grouped by sequences. We have added little shapes that show the triggering component (empty yellow circle), the start of a bullish trend (green circle) and the beginning of a bearish trend (red square). The trigger is the candlestick that blocks the way of a brand new square and forces the present trend to end.

When the catalyst component (empty yellow circle) stumbles on a candlestick, a stop is automatically triggered to put an end to the trend in order to start a fresh one. It can be an upward trend, identified by a green circle, or a downward trend, identified by a red square. It is an excellent system for traders who sell their bad position late and who are stubborn to keep it. Evaluate the effectiveness of the system on your own. The bullish and bearish signals conform quite closely to the cycle of the share.

Figure 5.10: Advanced Micro Devices and parabolic SAR

A stock market is composed of a bull and a bear cycles. These cycles usually have a minimal duration of three or four weeks. In the case of consolidation market, which moves sideways, or in an unstable market, this indicator could transmit many false signals. This is why you should always support your decisions through other indicators. Notice the small blue circle that highlights a simple square, isolated between two downtrends. That is unusual in a weekly chart.

> **TACTICS – Parabolic SAR.** It is recommended that you use the indicator for a weekly period unless the market shows an absence of volatility. Combine this indicator with another trend indicator such as MACD or ADX.

Force Index

The force index is an oscillator that measures the strength of bullish and bearish movements. The indicator is an unbounded indicator. The force index represents the multiplication of the volume of the day by the difference between the closing price of the day and the closing price of the previous day. This calculation allows you to highlight the trend as well as the strength of the trend. The indicator comes in the form of peaks with a central line of zero. An indicator below zero means a negative force, the bears are in control.

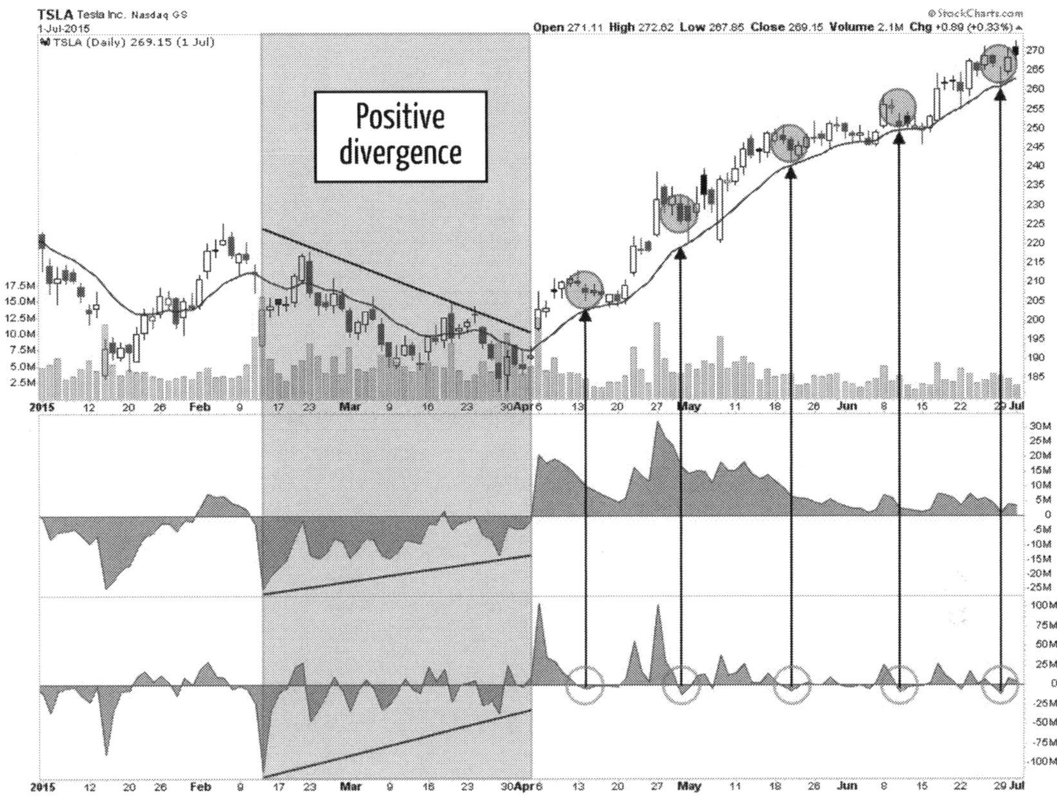

Figure 5.11: Tesla and the force index

An indicator above zero reveals a positive force, the bulls are in control. The particularity of this indicator is that it can be used in the short, medium and long term. You could use it with different averages to highlight the divergences and trends that may be drawn. We greatly recommend the use of 2-day and 13-day periods.

The figure 5.11 shows Tesla stock and two force indicators, a 2-day and a 13-day. Indicators significantly send the same signals except that they are more visible when set at two periods. The 13-day force index is smoother than the 2-day. Consider these basic rules when negotiating stocks based on the force index. Buy when the 2-day force index becomes negative during a positive trend of the 13-day force index. Make a short sale when the 2-day becomes positive during the negative trend of the 13-day force index. Consider the divergences. Buy when the prices decrease to a lower level while the force index reaches a higher low.

TACTICS – Force index. The force index helps determine if a stock's trend is strengthening or weakening. A 13-day force index moving higher, above zero, gives control to the bulls. A 13-day force index moving lower, below zero, gives control to the bears.

Chapter 6 – Momentum Indicators

Momentum indicators, or oscillators, represent reversal indicators, expect a change in a short space of time. These indicators respond quickly to different signals emitted by the stock and can highlight some dissonances or divergences. Your trading system must include at least one oscillator. Working exclusively with oscillators requires you to do day trading because these indicators react quickly to the movements of the market. Nowadays, the most popular oscillators are the Stochastic, the Relative Strength Index (RSI), the Rate of Change (ROC) and the Chaikin Money Flow.

Stochastic

The stochastic indicator was popularized in the late 1950s by Georges Lane. It is an oscillator that reacts rapidly, even before the stock price. There are several types of stochastic, and we pay attention to the slow stochastic, which offers fewer distortions than the fast stochastic. The stochastic tends to predict the turning points comparing the closing price of a stock to its price range of the period. This indicator is presented on a scale from 0 to 100. Two horizontal lines that serve as a threshold are shown in the background. The lower threshold is 20, and the upper threshold is 80. Most of the tools for chartists fix the average of 14 days. Two important rules result from this.

The first rule: when the stochastic passes below 20, the stock is oversold. It simply means that the stock price is too low compared to its historical price from the last 14 days. The immediate consequence should be to buy, but it is not so simple. The stochastic shows that the stock is oversold and has some potential to purchase, nothing more. That strictly means that the stock is low compared to its recent historical price; nothing proves that it could not fall anymore. We could even say that we buy a dropping value. It is better to wait patiently until the value stabilizes a bit and thinks about changing direction. It's preferable to buy when the stochastic passes over 20. This is an extremist indicator which acts quickly. It is a signal that incites investors to prepare for action.

The second rule: when the stochastic passes above 80, the stock is overbought. It simply means that the stock price is excessively high compared to its historical price from the last 14 days. The immediate consequence should be to liquidate, nothing more. Be prepared to act. Stochastic shows a stock that is potentially too expensive. The stochastic is made of two curves: a fast and a slow curve. It's the same principle as the MACD: the signal is bullish when the fast stochastic passes above the slow curve. The signal is bearish when the fast stochastic falls below the slow curve.

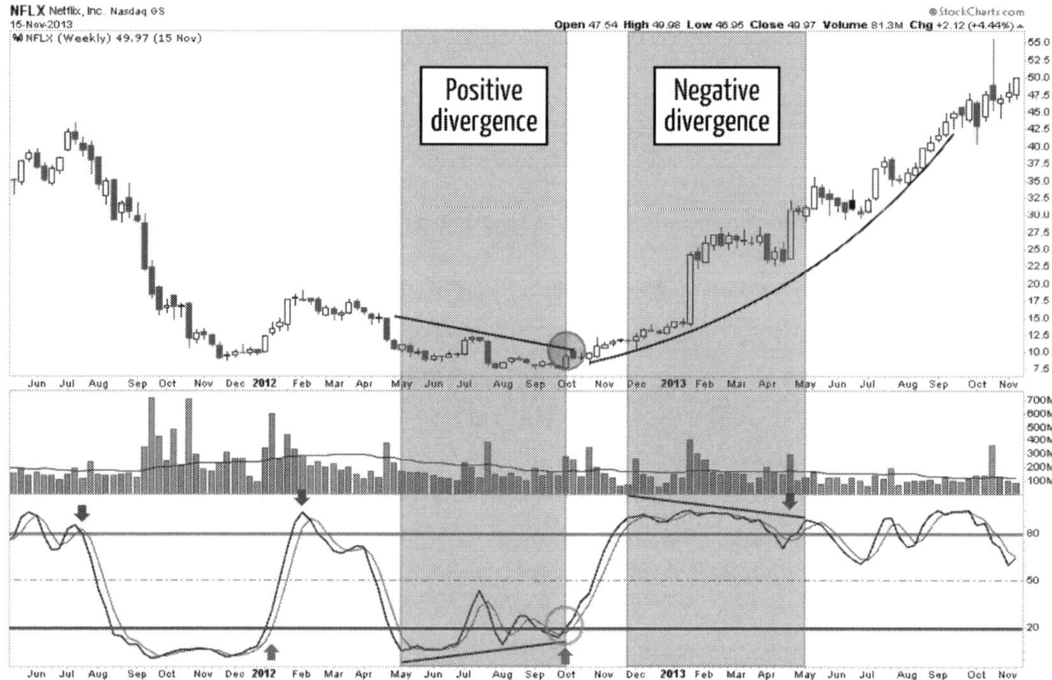

Figure 6.1: Netflix and stochastic

Look at the weekly chart of Netflix; there is much analysis to do. First of all, take a look at the arrows that present the direction changes triggered by the crossing of the slow and fast stochastic. The first three arrows gave excellent signals. Then pay attention to the first gray zone. A positive divergence is drawn to give a more powerful rally, making the stock go from $7.5 to $50 in 12 months. The stochastic has simply refused to reach a lower level and has crossed over 20 to launch an upward signal.

The second gray zone presents a negative divergence spread over six months. Throughout this period, the stock has not ceased to climb. To establish a trend, a parabolic line has been drawn under the stock price. It allows establishing an exit point at $47.50, while the crossing of the stochastic indicates a possible exit was set at $35. After analysis, we agree that this divergence sends a false signal. You should always use another indicator or a trend line to support your decision.

TACTICS – Stochastic. A stock that is overbought has strong chances of declining. A stock that is oversold is likely to rise. The divergences between the stochastic lines and the stock price mean a potential market reversal. During an uptrend, the stochastic tends to remain in an overbought situation, which **is not necessarily a sell signal.** In a downtrend, the stochastic tends to remain in an oversold situation, **which does not represent a buy signal.** Favor the stocks with an upward trend when the stochastic has come with an oversold level. It could be quite possible that the stock will make a slight drop before continuing to rise.

Relative Strength Index (RSI)

The Relative Strength Index (RSI) is an oscillator that measures the internal strength of a stock that sails between the threshold of 0 and 100. The upper zone, between 70 and 100, is an overbought zone and the lower area, between 0 and 30, is an oversold zone. It means that you should act in two zones. The 30–70 range is just a transition between the two main areas. By default, the number of periods is set at 14, but you can use other periods such as 5, 7, 9, 11 or 13. The situations when we use a period higher than 14 are unusual because the curve will be too smooth and respond slower to the price amplitudes. Also, RSI is useful for identifying divergences needed to anticipate the trends of different stocks or major indices.

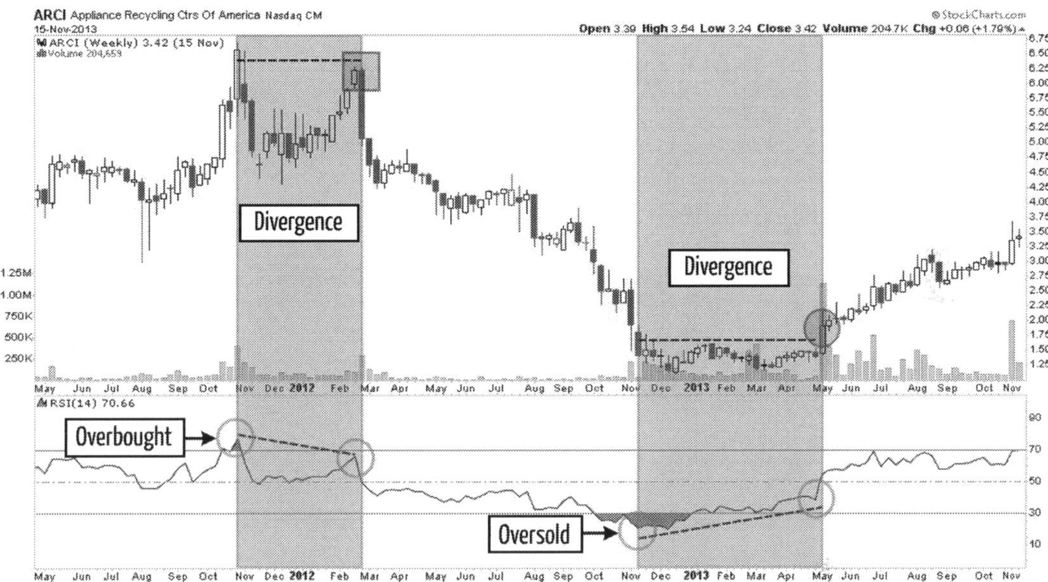

Figure 6.2: Appliance Recycling and RSI

Look at the relationship between the RSI and the stock price of Appliance Recycling. When the RSI is higher than 70 (overbought) or lower than 30 (oversold), it launches a potential reversal signal. This chart also shows two divergences between the RSI and the stock price. The first divergence is negative. RSI has been unable to make a new high. The second divergence is positive. RSI goes higher when the stock makes no progress. These divergences have been highly effective. Pay attention to the divergences that are being prepared in the overbought or oversold zones, as these are the most important to watch.

TACTICS – RSI. Set the bar higher for overbought and oversold situations. Use the target of 20–25 for the oversold and the target of 80–85 for the overbought. The indicator is useful in spotting the divergences that may announce changes in the trends for stock price or index. Pay less attention to the divergences within the 30–70 range.

Rate of Change (ROC)

The ROC is a momentum oscillator which allows measuring the progression speed of a stock. Its curve looks similar to the one of RSI, but axes are different. Two zones are present: a negative one and a positive one. The middle zone of the indicator is represented by zero, while the central level for the RSI is represented by the number 50. There is no upward or downward boundary.

ROC compares the closing price of the period with the one of another period (usually 12). ROC on the rise shows that the progression of the stock has been greater than the reference period. The share is overbought, and the upward trend is likely to continue. On the other hand, when the ROC is low, the stock is considered oversold, and the downward trend is expected to continue. The stock price tends to climb when the ROC is greater than zero. The share price tends to go down when the ROC dip below the zero level.

A stock that goes up while the ROC decreases indicates that a top is near. A stock that goes down while the ROC increases indicates that a new low is very close. Some providers of stock charts have a histogram instead of a curve. In addition, note that the scale of values of the ROC is different for every stock, which might be a little confusing.

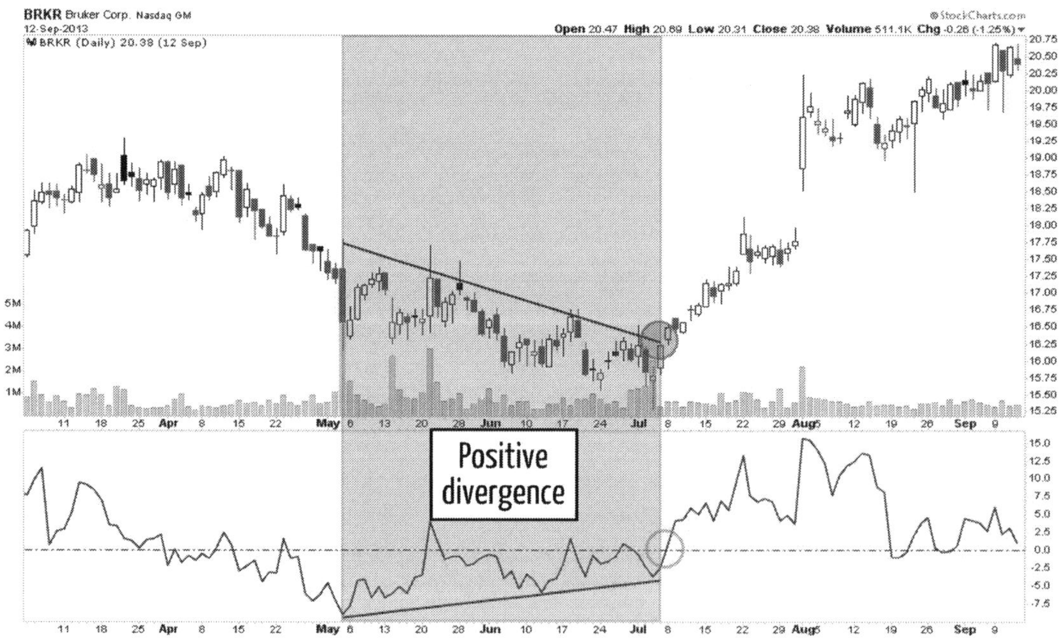

Figure 6.3: Bruker Corp and daily ROC

Use this indicator to locate the divergences that may affect the stock trend. As for the RSI, the more the divergences are distanced from the central area, the more weight they will have. Figure 6.3 illustrates the divergence between the ROC and the stock price of Bruker Corp. In early May, the ROC registered a low and continued its climb while the stock was falling. This situation indicates that a reversal is about to happen. At the beginning of July, the stock reached its lowest level of the last four months. Notice the volume associated with this bottom. There was panic among the sellers, and the buyers took advantage of this chance to buy cheap.

Figure 6.4: Bruker Corp and weekly ROC

The figure above illustrates the weekly chart of Bruker Corp. Notice the divergences predicting the trend reversals. In addition, pay attention to the vertical scale of the ROC, which is quite different from that of the daily chart shown in figure 6.3. This representation requires us to invent landmarks for every stock because the scale is not static like in RSI or stochastic. A buy signal is generated following a positive divergence. A sell signal is generated following a negative divergence.

> **TACTICS – ROC.** The more the indicator rises above the equilibrium level, the more the stock is overbought. The more the stock falls below the equilibrium level, the more the stock is oversold. This indicator is useful for locating the divergences that may set changes in trends of a stock or index. The RSI indicator presents a better alternative because the axes have the same threshold for all the stocks.

Chaikin Money Flow

The Chaikin Money Flow has been developed by Marc Chaikin. This indicator is different from other momentum indicators by the fact that combines the price and volume, while most indicators of momentum base their calculations only on price. It's an indicator of an indicator because it bases its calculations on the Accumulation/Distribution indicator. It makes two comparisons. Firstly, it compares the closing price with the high/low range. Secondly, it compares the result obtained with total volume for the same interval.

When the Chaikin Money Flow is above zero, it indicates that we are in a period of accumulation. When the Chaikin Money Flow is less than zero, this indicates that we are in a period of distribution. The farther the indicator is from zero, the more important the strength of the signal. It allows you to highlight pressure on a buyer or seller related to a share. This indicator will be positive when prices regularly close near their top. The result is a signal of strength. It will be negative if the stock price regularly closes at the lowest level. This is a weak signal.

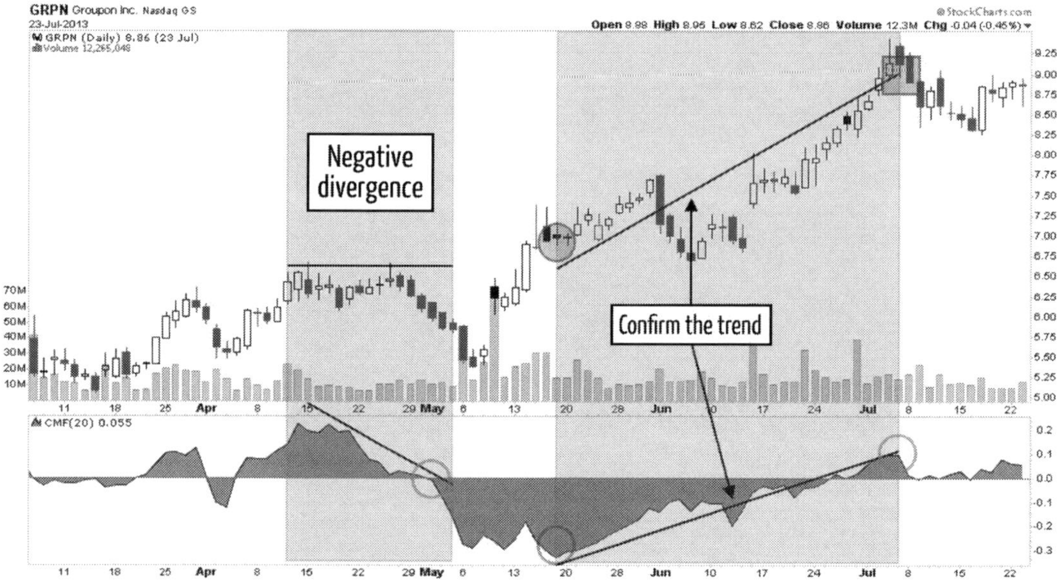

Figure 6.5: Groupon and Chaikin money flow

Look at the daily chart of Groupon. First of all, a negative divergence is well announced by the Chaikin Money Flow. The indicator falls below the threshold of zero. Secondly, in late May, note the support given to the stock price through the indicator. Since the stock always closes near the previous close, this accentuates the pressure on the buyer and involves an increase of the Chaikin Money Flow. In early July, buying pressure is reduced, and it brings the Chaikin Money Flow back in a well-balanced position.

TACTICS – Chaikin Money Flow. This indicator shows an interesting way to detect accumulation and distribution phases. Divergences between the indicator and prices can provide valuable insights into their own evolution of the trend that begins to take shape.

Chapter 7 – Volatility Indicators

The volatility indicators reflect the change in stock price. The wider the stock gaps, the more powerful the volatility index will be. Volatility increases when the stock price fluctuates in a wider range of value. A share with modest volatility announces a weak amplitude of the stock price. The volatility of a stock has nothing to do with the trend but rather with the amplitude of the upward or downward movement.

Bollinger Bands

This indicator appears in the form of an envelope whose middle is a 20-period SMA. The bands correspond to an upper and lower margin based on the SMA. The spacing of the bands shows the volatility level in a stock or an indicator. The more bands are discarded, the more volatility is present. When the share price exceeds the envelope, this indicates a potential turnaround. In addition to being an indicator of volatility, the Bollinger bands show the direction of the trend after a congestion zone.

Some financial strategists recommend monitoring all exits of the lower band and taking action the next day when it is obvious that the stock will close higher than the day before. There is no way to know if the selling pressure will continue after this rebound. Let's look at the example below. The eBay stock generated ten exits of the lower band during February and March before a major turnaround, which began March 18.

Figure 7.1: eBay and the Bollinger bands

To better ensure you're covered, invest when the stock passes over the dotted median line. As is shown in figure 7.1, eBbay does not remain bullish for a long time, but it allows a small 5% return twice in April and May. Do not make any investment decision based simply on the fact that the share is outside the Bollinger bands.

The greatest strength of the Bollinger bands resides in their use on a weekly basis. Monitor securities whose envelope shrinks significantly. Taken alone, the contraction means lack of volatility. However, this indicates that a significant event will happen in the short or medium term, upward and downward, one that we are unable to predict for the moment.

Figure 7.2: SunPower and a bullish expansion of the Bollinger bands

Watch the explosion generated in December 2012 by the bullish expansion of the Bollinger bands on the SunPower stock from figure 7.2. The bands gradually contracted for 12 months before widening again. The stock exploded in December 2012 from $4 to $20 in less than six months.

> **TACTICS – Bollinger bands.** Combined with other indicators, the Bollinger bands is an indicator of choice in your trading system. Consider investing only when the stock passes above the median band. Furthermore, go long when the median is upward. Monitor the contractions of the bands. They announce a change in trend that could be explosive.

Average True Range (ATR)

The Average True Range is an excellent indicator for measuring the volatility of a stock. This indicator does not detect the direction or the market trend. Rather, ATR is an unbounded indicator which allows measuring the investor interest in a stock or index. It measures the average between the highest and the lowest levels. A high ATR indicates steep volatility, and a low ATR indicates a soft volatility level. When the indicator has low variation during a certain period, this suggests that stock price is in a narrow trading range. Periods of low volatility announce violent movements in prices. When the ATR presents higher levels, up or down, it suggests a possible trend reversal. Draw trend lines to estimate an entry or an exit point. This point of entry or exit may be the beginning of a new explosive trend.

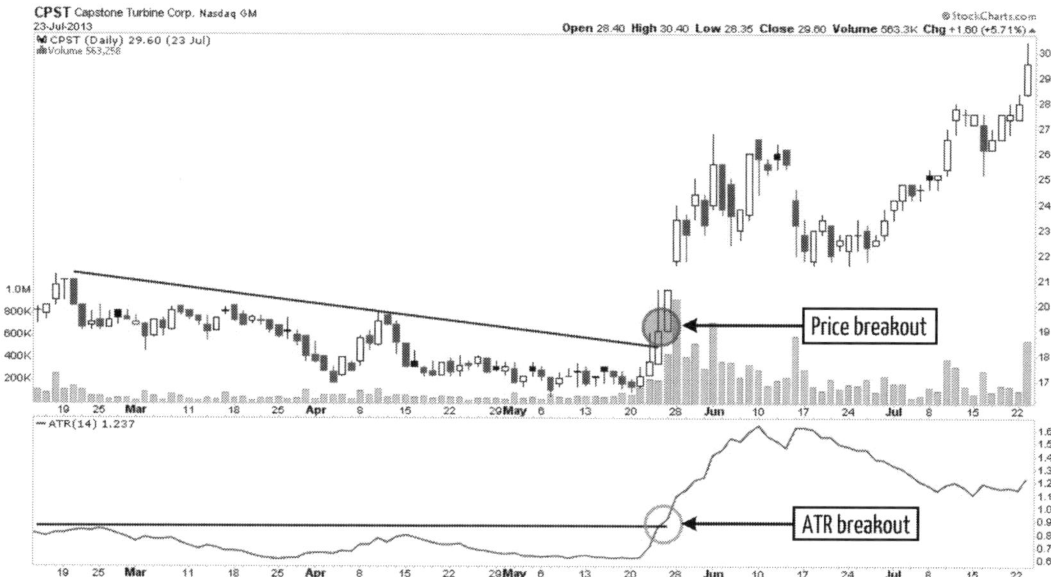

Figure 7.3: Capstone Turbide and ATR

The figure above highlights the relationship between the ATR and the stock price. Look at the volume; the absence of new buyers pulls the stock lower. The period of low volatility from February to May prepared us for a possible change of direction of the share price. During the ATR's trend breakout, there is an increase of 50% for Capstone Turbide.

> **TACTICS – Average True Range.** Periods of low volatility precede bull and bear movements. The high interest of investors does not necessarily mean that the trend is about to reverse.

Chapter 8 – Volume Indicators

The main indicators are based on stock price and also on stock volume. Volume indicators are mainly used to confirm trends and launch an alert of a possible trend reversal. The volume is linked to the trend. The emotional implications of traders have to materialize through volumes. In this chapter, we will talk about the indicators that directly come from the volume and offer the possibility of increasing bullish or bearish signals. These indicators have been developed to help in decision-making and to furnish more explicit signals.

Volume

This indicator shows the number of transactions exchanged by periods (minutes, hours, days, weeks, etc.). For many traders, the volume is the only indicator used to make a good buying decision. It is logical. Other technical indicators constantly use the volume in their formulas. The volume is the basis of technical analysis. An increase in the price of a share with strong volumes indicates that this increase is approved by the markets. A decrease in stock price with high volumes indicates that the decrease is also confirmed by markets.

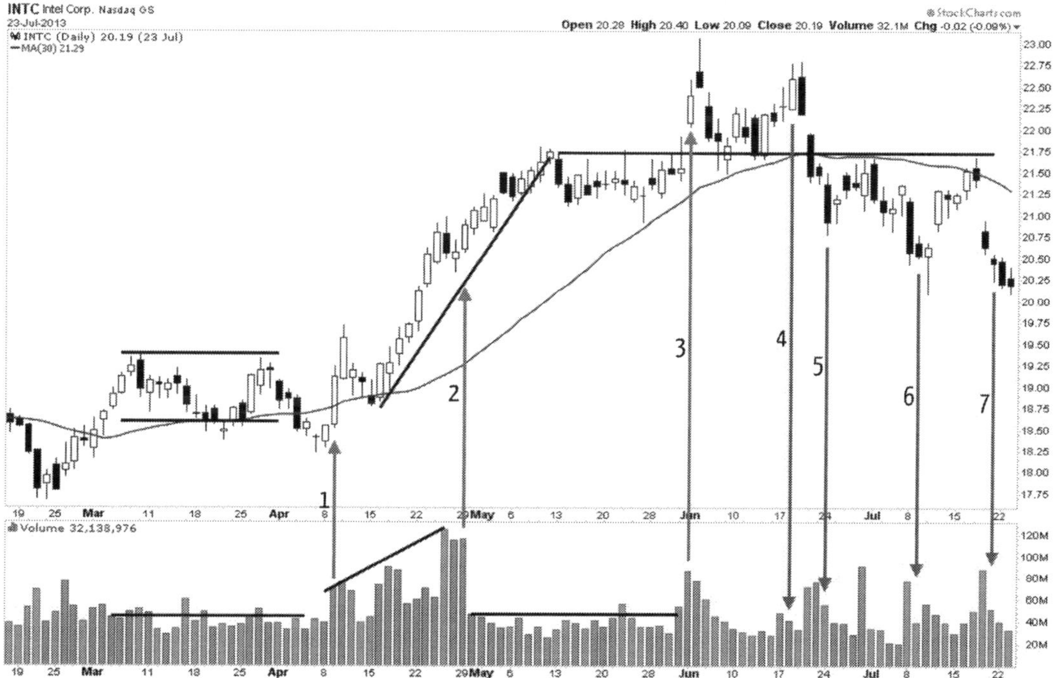

Figure 8.1: Intel Corp and volume.

The preceding figure provides much information through the volumes of Intel Corp. A moving average was added to make a rapprochement with stages seen before. Each day has its volume bar, a gray bar for the days when the stock price is rising and a red bar for the days of decline. We have also drawn trend lines. Here are seven important points connected to the volumes for Intel chart:

Point 1

The stock has just ended a consolidation period with a fairly stable volume level. It completes its stage 1. The volume level is increasing. The stock comes out of the trend channel and breaks its SMA30 and crossover trend channel.

Point 2

The stock is in stage 2. The positive trend is supported by a significant increase in the volume of transactions. An uptrend must be supported by a strong volume. The volume drops rapidly during this stage, which could have damaged the duration of this upward movement.

Point 3

We are in stage 3, which is the consolidation stage. The volume level is lower, except for temporary revival. The stock registers an increase in the volume level lower than the one in stage 2.

Point 4

Breaking stage 3 and breaking the SMA30, stage 4 is taking shape. Some buyers believe that the boost will continue and do not want to miss their chance to make fabulous profits.

Point 5

The stock collapses even more but comes back to test the support area. There is a significant volume increase, which is not obligatory during a stage 3 breakdown. In a bearish panic situation, volumes can greatly increase.

Point 6

The buyers are testing the support zone. The volume peaks are irregular. Future losers have just entered the game.

Point 7

It comes to the final test of the resistance/support area. Sellers abdicate, the volume increases and stage 4 continues.

Intraday Volume

Experience will allow you to observe that there are two moments in the day when the activity level is highest: opening and closing of the markets. Many traders only put their energies at the beginning and at the end of a session because it is precisely there that we find the greatest variations in the price of a stock. The midday portion usually offers less volatility and volume.

Look at the figure 8.2 and pay attention to the parabolic distribution of volume for a few days. The volume is higher in the beginning and at the end of a session than in the middle of the day.

We see that the first half-hour provides the highest volume level of the day. The stock price reached in the first half-hour could not be surpassed for the rest of the day. The volume decrease in the midday is caused by the market makers who step out of the office for lunch.

Figure 8.2: Facebook intraday volume

Volume by Price

This indicator shows the volume associated with different price levels. It is represented by the horizontal bars which act as support and resistance at distinct price levels. The bars are based on the required period. For example, for a five-year weekly chart, the bars represent the data during the five years. The longer the bar, the more significant the support/resistance level will be.

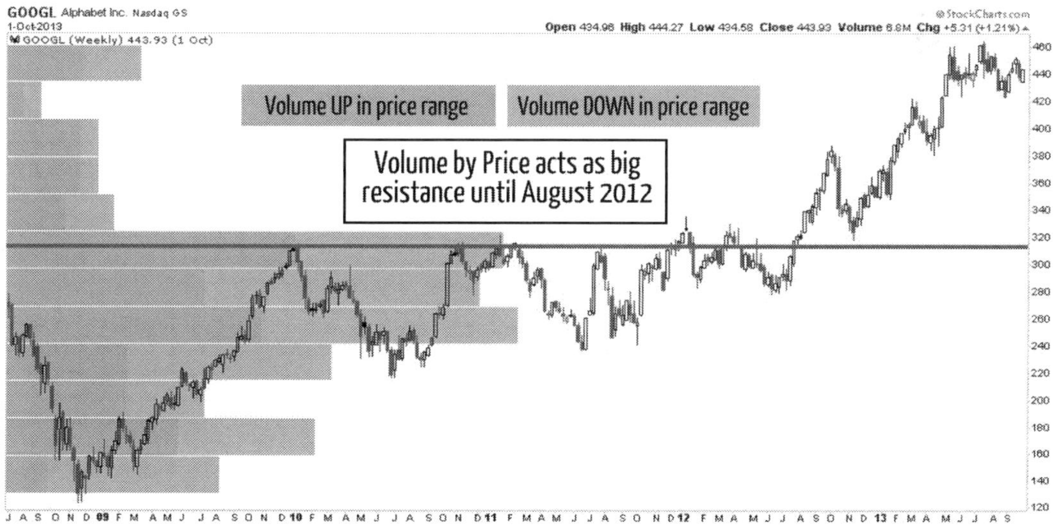

Figure 8.3: Google and Volume by price indicator

The preceding chart of Google shows that level of $315 was a resistance and became the support after August 2012. We can agree that, in the event of the fall of this stock, it could return to that $315 level since this support had been raised for three years. The use of this indicator, among others, predicts the limits that the stock could bounce. All data are taken into consideration for the required period. It's implied that the most important support level revealed for this five-year chart could be different for a chart covering the last six months. It is necessary to have a portrait of volume by price on a weekly and daily time frame.

TACTICS – Volume by price. Use the bars of the volume by price to anticipate areas of support and resistance on which stock price could bounce. Draw the most important support and resistance lines. Work on daily and weekly chart to determine key levels. Consider this indicator as a fundamental element of your technical analysis system.

Accumulation/Distribution

This indicator allows you to isolate phases of accumulation and distribution. It is a useful indicator for confirming current trends. When the indicator is placed in a positive trend, meaning higher highs and higher lows, the stock is in a period of accumulation. Conversely, the stock is in a distribution period when the curve is in a downtrend, which means lower highs and lows. Use this indicator to confirm the trend of the share price.

Equally, learn to spot the divergences between the Accumulation/Distribution curve and the stock price. The divergence sends a potential reversal signal. A divergence is bullish when prices are in a downward trend while the indicator is ascendant. A divergence is bearish when prices are in an uptrend while the indicator is in a downtrend.

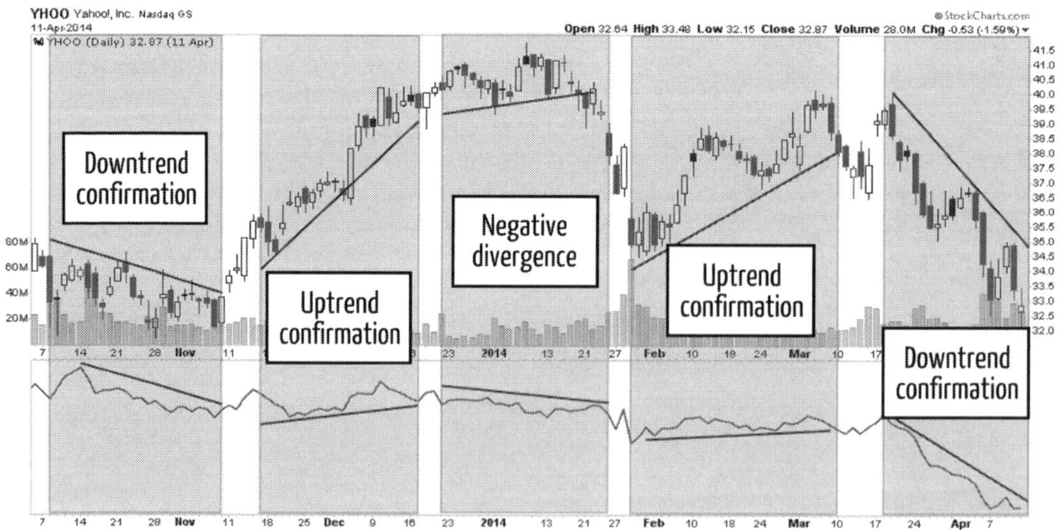

Figure 8.4: Yahoo and Accumulation/Distribution indicator

The above chart of Yahoo presents four confirmations of the trend supported by the Accumulation/Distribution curve: two uptrends and two downtrends. These confirmations allow an investor to add weight to his decision of investing during the increase or short selling while the stock decline. Pay particular attention to stocks that have a long accumulation period. There is a chance that a resistance break can generate a strong buy signal. These stocks have a huge potential, but the wait can be quite long. Your patience could be put through a tough test.

Observe that the volume weight is more significant on the highest price of the shares than on the lowest price. The central zone presents a divergence between the Accumulation/Distribution and the share price. The stock is unable to close higher while the Accumulation/Distribution drops during four weeks. This divergence announces the probable appearance—or the possibility—of coming decline. That is precisely what happened in late January.

> **TACTICS – Accumulation/Distribution.** This indicator can be used to confirm an uptrend or a downtrend. It is useful in spotting divergences that may announce changes in the trend of stock.

On Balance Volume (OBV)

On Balance Volume, or OBV, is an indicator with no threshold, which means that it does not have any scales. The OBV is a net volume accumulator. When the price closes above the preceding closing price, volume is added to the OBV of the day. When the price closes below the previous closing price, we subtract the volume from the OBV of the day.

Figure 8.5: eBay and On balance volume.

This indicator allows you to separate phases of accumulation and distribution. It is a useful indicator for highlighting divergences and confirming current trends. The OBV confirms a positive trend when the ups and downs are often higher. The OBV confirms a downward trend when the highs and lows are much lower.

The OBV indicator compares the entries and the exits of a stock with its volume. The steady increase in stock price should normally be supported at least by a constant volume. Without the support of the volumes, the stock price will eventually fall. Beyond the divergence detection, the OBV allows determining the entry points during the trend reversal. The downward trend break of the OBV indicates that you should buy eBay in early 2012 even before the stock started its extraordinary rise. See how the OBV has supported the rising of the share for 18 months.

TACTICS – On balance volume. OBV indicator serves to confirm an uptrend or a downtrend. The indicator is useful in spotting the divergences that may announce trend changes in stock or index. Pull trend lines and pay attention to the breaking targets. They can announce beautiful reversals.

Chapter 9 – Continuation Patterns

Patterns are indispensable from the arsenal of a chartist. Generally, patterns can be grouped as either reversal patterns or continuation patterns. Continuation patterns refer to configurations that mark a pause during a trend. These breaks are consolidation periods which will allow the stock to continue its trend with the same vigor and often in a more explosive way. These patterns are numerous and can be recognized by many traders and even by software and trading tools.

Cup and Handle

The Cup and handle was discovered and put forward by William J. O'Neil in his book *How to Make Money in Stocks.* The Cup and Handle is usually the continuation of a bullish trend. This pattern is made of two rounded bottoms. The first bottom, deeper, represents the cup, while the second bottom represents the handle.

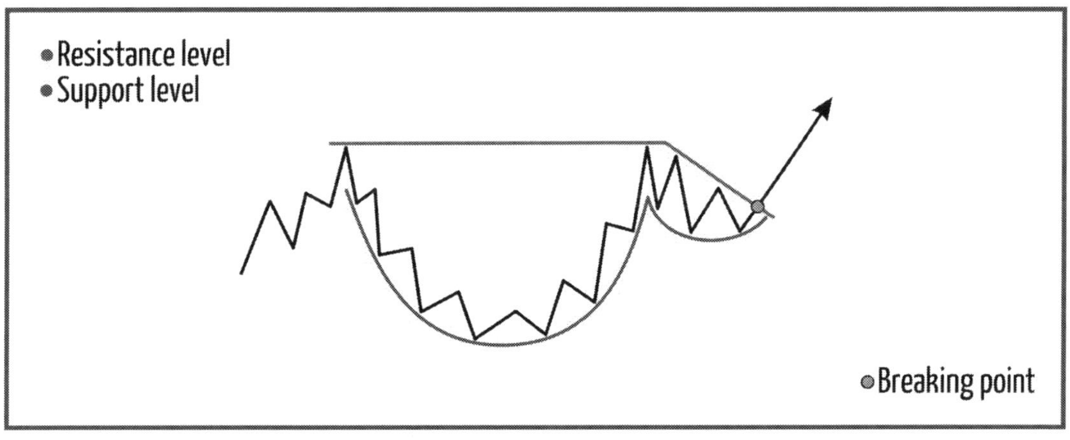

Figure 9.1: The Cup and handle pattern remains very efficient on breakout with strong volumes. After spotting a stock with this kind of configuration on a weekly chart, place it on a watchlist. It is likely to generate significant gains.

The primary bottom draws the neckline and the resistance threshold. The second bottom, smaller and more concentrated, ends with a breakout coupled with a relevant increase in the volume. As in any breakout, the volume stays the most significant factor to monitor. Without any volume increase, the break of the resistance line is almost impossible.

The figure 9.2 shows the Cup and Handle generated by Noah Holdings. The pattern extends on over 14 months. It adds even more weight to the breakout that occurred in May 2013. A neckline at $8.25 appears in October 2011. The first bottom extends over a period of 12 months. During this period, no attempt to test resistance was made. In March 2013, a pullback was performed under the neckline to draw the second bottom, a smaller one. The objective is equivalent to the difference between the neckline and the lowest level of the first bottom.

Figure 9.2: Noah Holdings and a Cup and Handle

Cup and handle is one of the most winning figures, with a success rate between 70% and 80%. Give priority to the signals generated on a weekly chart. When you have the chance to detect one, monitor it closely because it offers significant potential gains.

Dead-Cat Bounce

The term 'Dead-Cat Bounce' comes from the idea that even when dead, a cat will bounce back if it falls. The rebound will not be as high as if the cat had been living. The same thing happens in the stock market. A stock that suffers from a decline will finish, sooner or later, by a reversal to the upside. It's the same for any stock.

Quite often, this configuration begins with a huge downward gap which follows the publication of bad economic news. A fast bounce back of a stock is rare. This configuration is a trend continuation pattern. The downward trend should follow a light bounce back. The highest impulse represents the 'cat bounce.'

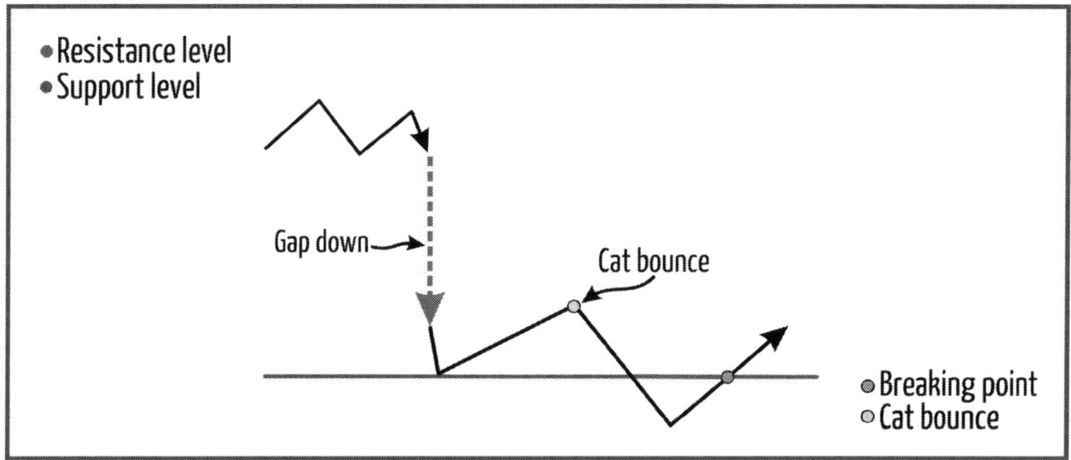

Figure 9.3: The Dead-Cat Bounce pattern is a passive model. It refers to a past event where the premises cannot be predicted. The sharp drop at the market opening is often due to bad economic news related to the stock. It may take up to 12 months to close the gap.

This reversal of the situation could be temporary. The period of consolidation typically ranges from 2 to 12 months. At best, you can expect to earn from 10% to 15% on the rebound. Place this stock on your watchlist. The breakout of the resistance line will be your first buy signal.

Figure 9.4: Fortinet and a Dead-Cat Bounce

The above chart of Fortinet shows a 30% drop of the stock from its summit in March. The share price stabilizes and rebounds by 10%. It is the dead-cat bounce. Consequently, the stock comes back to the bounce area and breaks this support zone later. This last capitulation offers munitions, and the stock goes up rapidly, as the pros smelled a good opportunity. There are chances to close the initial gap on this climb.

Triangle – Ascending Triangle

The ascending triangle is a continuation pattern with an upward trend. It is the most popular pattern among traders as well as one of the most present on the stock market. This pattern represents an intermediate phase, a pause in a rising trend. The ascending triangle is represented by a horizontal line—the resistance over which the stock price stumbles—and by a diagonal, which offers the support. As time passes, the stock price rises back towards the resistance level, and it breaks it with strong volumes. This pattern still sends many false signals that cause significant losses to investors.

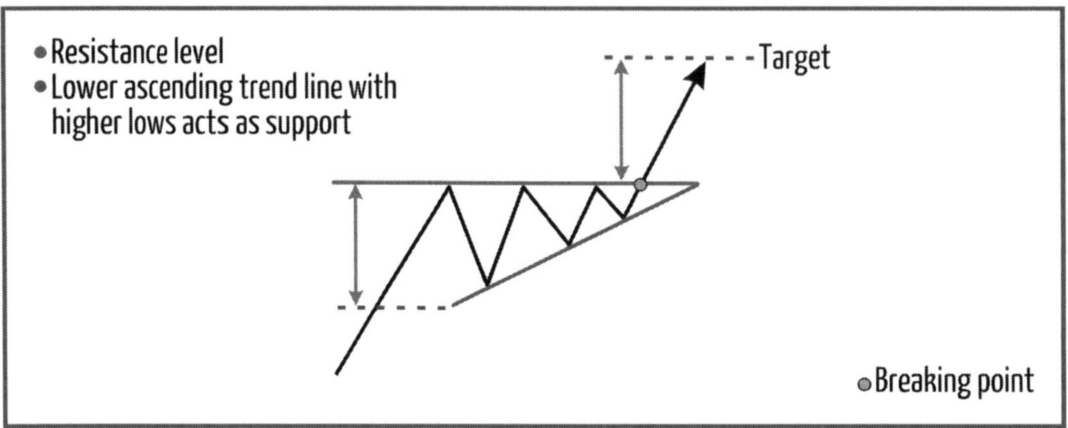

Figure 9.5: The Ascending Triangle is a pattern very valued by a lot of investors. Closely monitor the stocks that have tested the resistance line several times before. The break could generate big profits

We can never repeat enough that it is essential to have a strong volume on the resistance break. This volume must be three to five times higher than the average volume of the last 30 periods. Without this condition, you expose yourself to a potential quick reversal which may lead to significant losses. Two groups are opposed when handling this model. The pros sell when the stock reaches its resistance, and dummies buy hoping for an upward break of the prices.

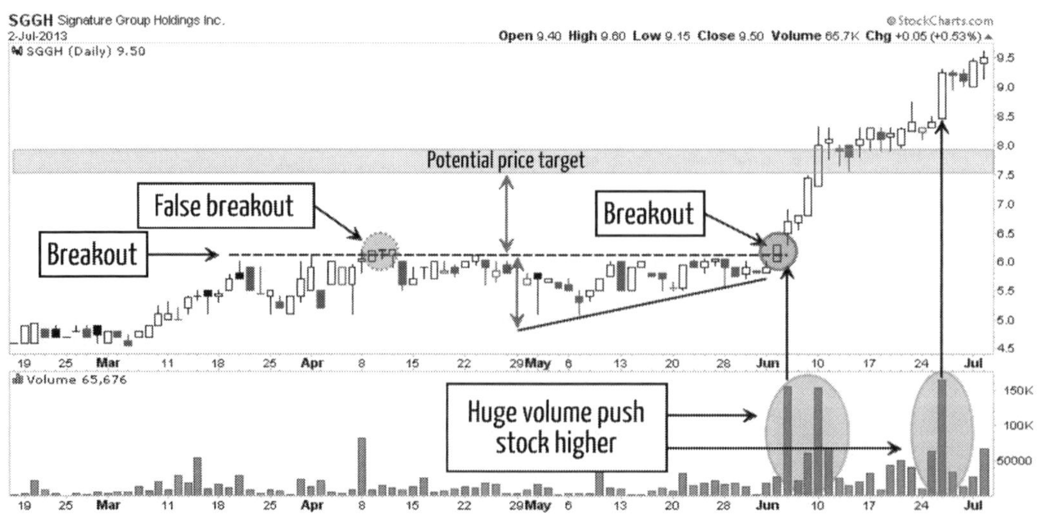

Figure 9.6: Signature Group Holdings and an Ascending Triangle

Pros could sell everything just above the break when they realize that the volume does not meet expectations. They take advantage of this false signal to do a short sale, suspecting that the stock will return to the downward trend rapidly. The potential target is equivalent to the vertical height of the triangle added to the resistance level. This target remains approximate. A triangle with a minimum of 20 periods is required to generate a solid pattern. To be valid, the two lines forming the triangle must be touched three times by the candlesticks.

Pay attention to the figure 9.6 and look at the number of times that the share price of Signature Group Holdings tests the resistance line representing the top of the triangle. The tests, prior to the formation of the triangle, would have shaped an extremely powerful breakout. Now, pay attention to the false breakout signal identified by a blue circle. First, the breakout is not sufficient to confirm the breakout. Furthermore, no volume increase has come to sustain this resistance break.

Several experts suggest that the breakout should be at 2/3 of the triangle, before the two lines of the triangle would touch each other. A break at 2/3 would indicate that the buyers had won the fight and were hastening to continue. Figures 9.6 and 9.7 tend to confirm this theory. However, the most important element remains the volume power.

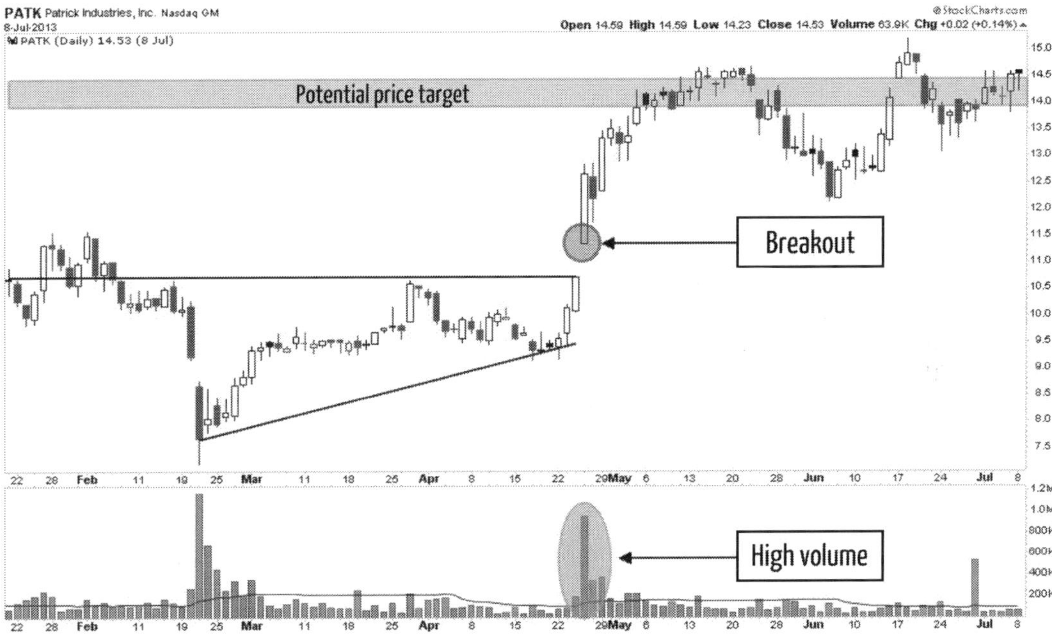

Figure 9.7: Patrick Industries and an Ascending Triangle

The chart of Patrick Industries shows an upward triangle built in an irregular way extended over 40 days. The stock price tested the resistance twice at halfway. In late April, the volume strength of the breakout is unequivocal. We assist to a strong break built in a period of more than two months. The volume is equivalent to at least ten times the average volume of the previous 30 days. During such an increase, it is quite natural to observe the appearance of a gap. This gap launches a signal to the markets that the stock is undervalued, draining many investors to new highs.

Triangle – Descending Triangle

Opposite to the ascending triangle, the descending triangle is a bearish continuation pattern. It stands for an intermediary phase, a pause in a downward trend. The descending triangle is formed by a horizontal line that represents the support on which the stock price rebounds and a diagonal representing the declining resistance. Two groups are opposed: the pros sell when the stock reaches its resistance, and the dummies buy, hoping for an upward break of the prices.

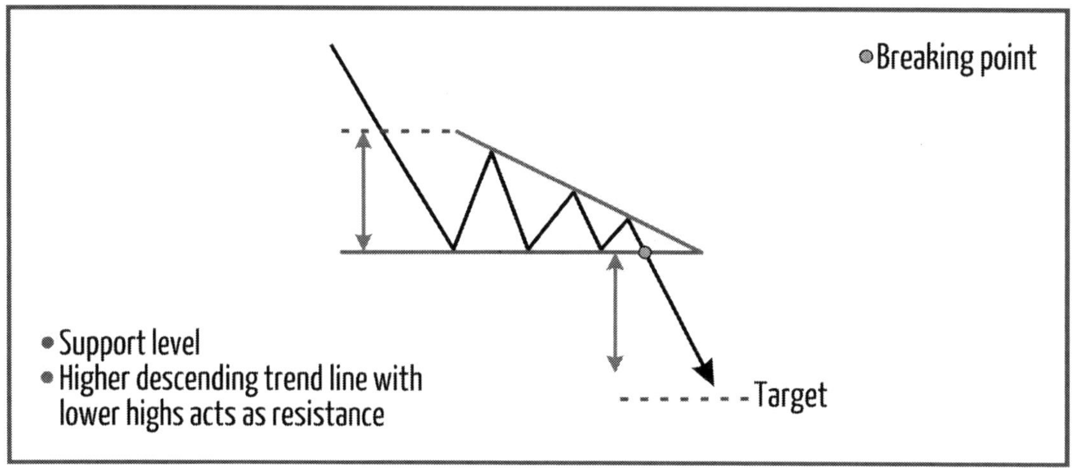

Figure 9.8: Descending Triangle pattern. This model is very effective. If you are invested, think about selling your stock, because the fall is predictable.

The mood is bad; the stock received some negative guidance. As time passes by, the stock price decreases and just breaks the support level. It's not required to have an increase in volume during the breakdown. The potential target is equivalent to the vertical height of the triangle subtracted from the support line. This target remains approximate.

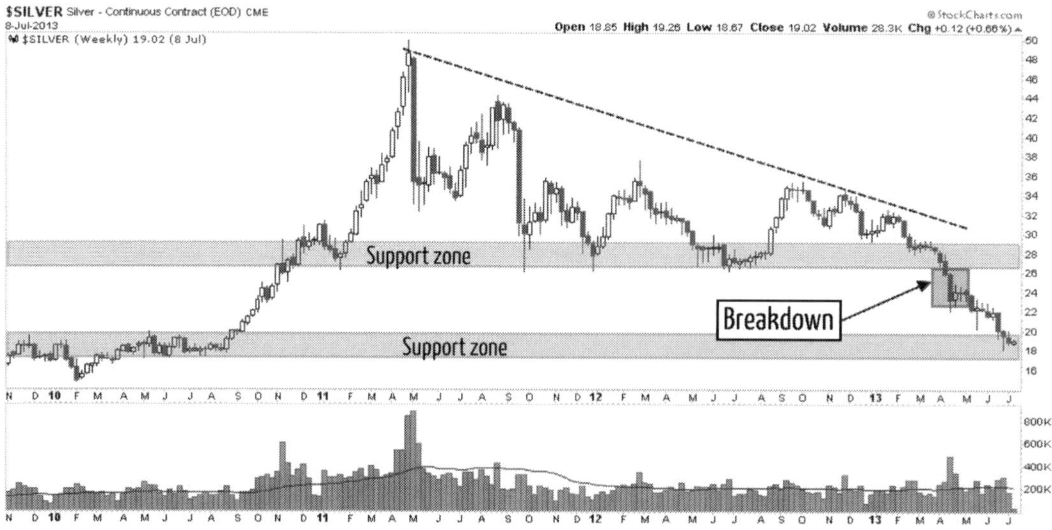

Figure 9.9: Silver and a Descending Triangle

The figure 9.9 illustrates a beautiful descending triangle for silver. The descending triangle extends over two years. To be valid, the two lines that shape the triangle should be touched at least three times by the candlesticks. We can consider a possible target of $7.5 for the stock price ($27.5-[$47.5-$27.5]). Think about another zone of support between $17.50 and $20. The target of $7.5 remains highly exaggerated. Notice the slight increase in volume during the break of the $27.5 support zone. As any breakout, the downward break of the triangle should appear at 2/3 of the triangle, which means before the two lines of the triangle touch each other. A break at 2/3 would indicate that the sellers had won the battle and were eager to continue the fight.

Bull Flag and Pennant

The bullish flag and the pennant are continuation patterns found at rallies supported by the strong fundamental news. The flag and the pennant are favorable breaks in the pursuit of a stock's upward trend. This pause is beneficial and creates a comfort zone. The transition period is marked by a lower volume just before the stock begins to fly on strong volume.

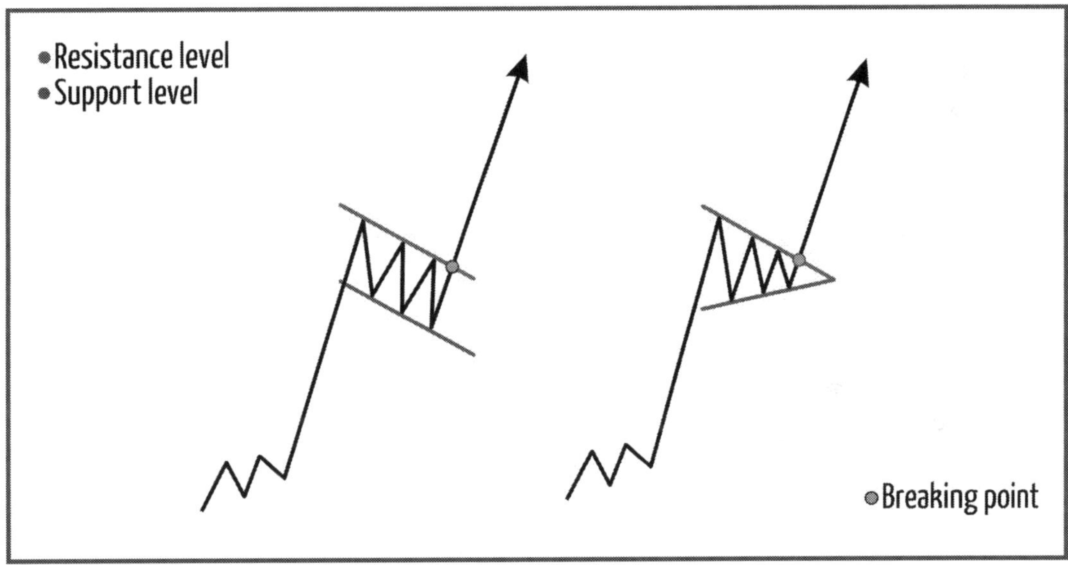

Figure 9.10: Bullish flag and pennant patterns in an uptrend. In an upward continuation, the downward flag leads to less indecision than the pennant. The latter is a smaller replica of the symmetrical triangle which is a pattern of indecision that may lead the stock higher or lower.

A downward flag in an upward continuation is perceived as a bullish signal and as an indication that the previous rising trend will continue. After a sudden and steep price climb, a flag reflects a temporary pause in the ascending trend, consisting of two parallel trend lines that draw the shape of a rectangular flag. The flag has a downward trend which seems to go against the tide. Favor the flags that last between 12 and 20 days. A longer duration invalidates the pattern.

Figure 9.11: Pfizer and Bullish Flag in an upward trend

The figure above illustrates a downward flag in an upward continuation. Some investors had sold when the stock began its decline in the early part of December. However, new investors accumulate, hoping it will rise further. As the symmetrical triangle, the pennant is a wavering pattern that is built with two converging lines, one for support and the other serving as resistance.

After a sudden increase and price accentuation, a pennant reflects a temporary pause in the upward trend. Favor the pennants with durations of 20 days or fewer. If the duration is over 20 periods, you are in front of a symmetrical triangle whose trend, upward or downward, often remains unpredictable.

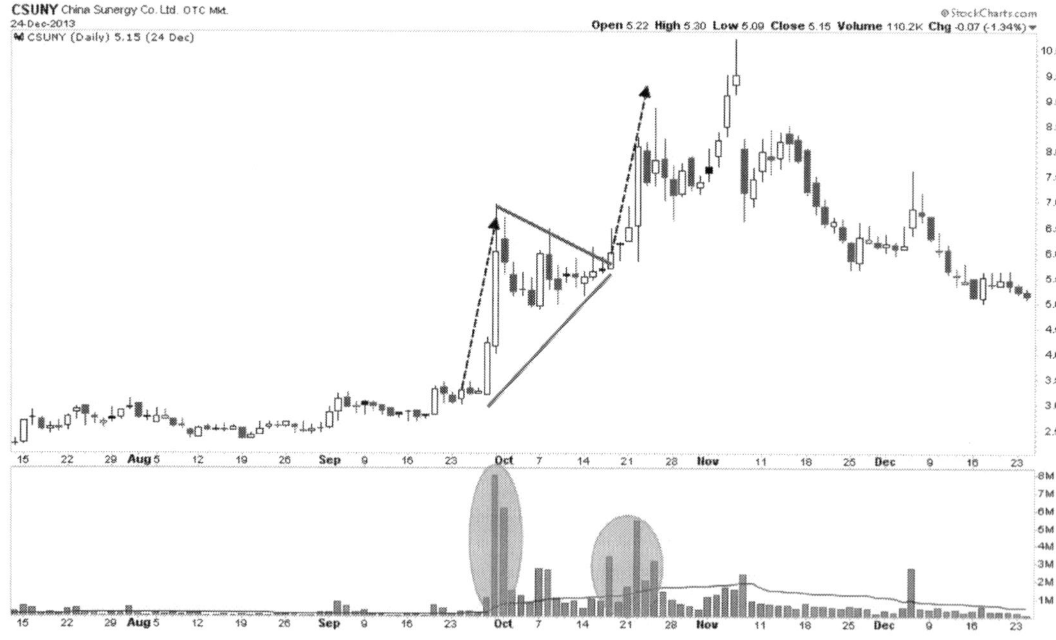

Figure 9.12: China Sunergy and a Bullish Pennant

The figure 9.12 illustrates a pennant in an ascending continuation for China Sunergy. Note the volume increase in late September is well superior to the days that precede the upward break of the resistance. The first increase in volume suggests another leg of growth starting in late October. The sudden volume rise adds more vigor to the increase of the stock price, which doubled in two weeks.

Bear Flag and Pennant

The bear flag and pennant are patterns found during a downward trend. The fall happens in two phases interrupted by a momentary pause. The sharp drop is often caused by bad news referring to the stock. This transition period is marked by a lower volume just before the stock drops again. You should know that these different models are not 100 percent guaranteed. The patterns could get destroyed at the midpoint of their realization. Some economic news, the arrival of further investors or technology improvement by a competitor could influence the stock price. Technical analysis cannot predict all external variables to the share; please take note.

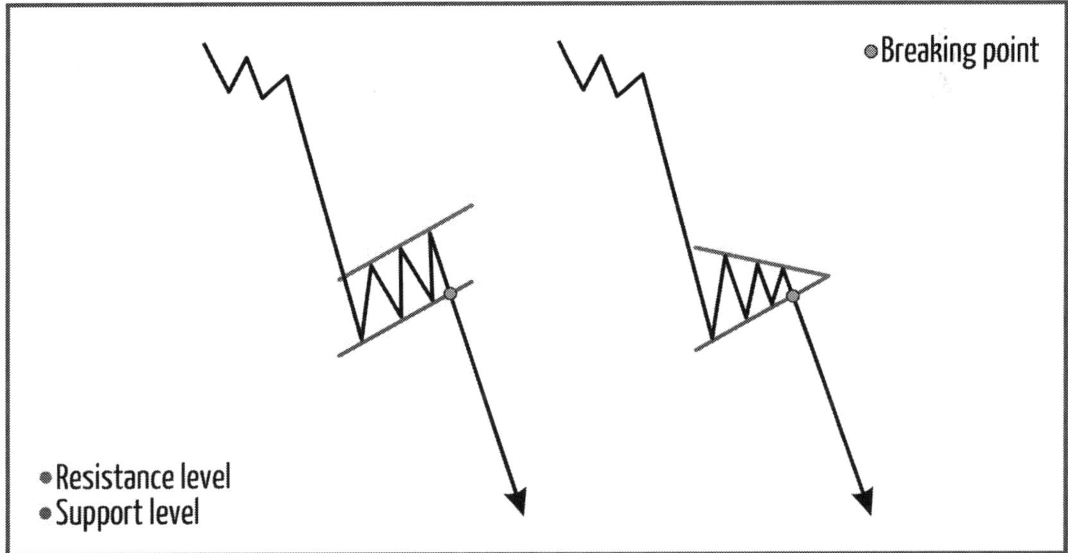

Figure 9.13: Bear Flag and Pennant patterns in a downtrend. The upward flag in a bearish trend provides less indecision as the pennant. The latter is a smaller replica of the symmetrical triangle, which is an indecision pattern.

An upward flag in a declining continuation is perceived as a bearish signal and as an indication that the previous downward trend will continue. After a steep descent of the stock price, a flag reflects a temporary pause in the sliding trend, consisting of two parallel trend lines that form a rectangular flag. This flag has an upward trend that seems to go against the wave. Favor the flags that last 20 days or less. Past this time, the pattern is invalid.

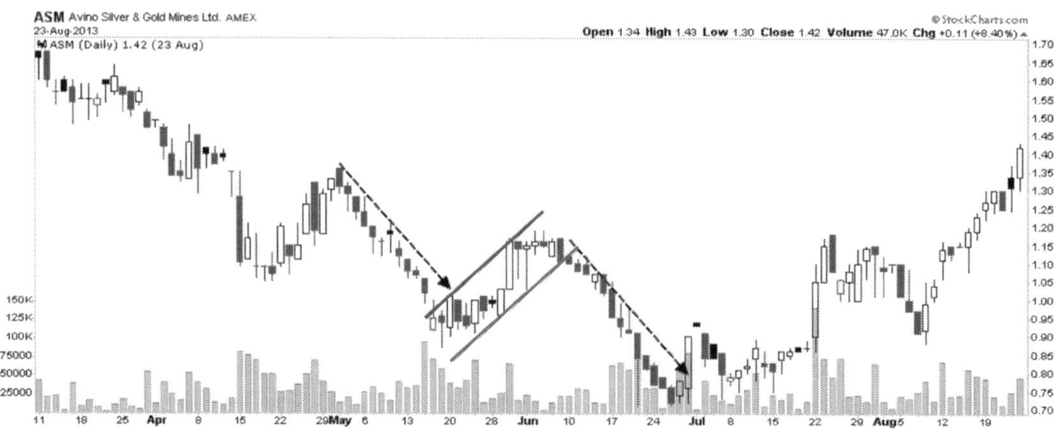

Figure 9.14: Avino Silver & Gold Mines and a bearish flag. This figure shows a downward trend of Avino Silver from May to July, broken by a bullish flag. Note the symmetry of the slumps identified through the black arrows

Bullish or Falling Wedge

A falling wedge usually marks a pause in an uptrend. The stock leaps within a range dominated by support and resistance. The range has the shape of a triangle with the slope oriented towards the bottom. The contraction of the triangle's extremity means a future breakout. A consensus emerged between the buyers and sellers before the upward trend came back even stronger.

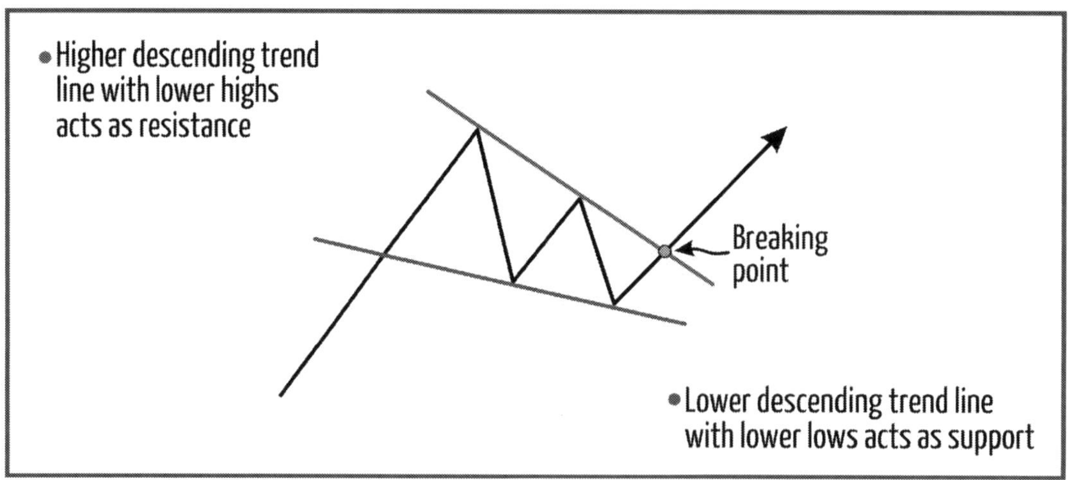

Figure 9.15: Bullish or Falling Wedge. The falling wedge allows anticipating an upward break of the stock. The break on high volume is required and reassures the investors.

The length of the leg before the formation of the triangle is used to anticipate the length of the second rise. Symmetry between the two increases is quite frequent. However, the increase could present small traps, and the rise will not necessarily be made in a straight line.

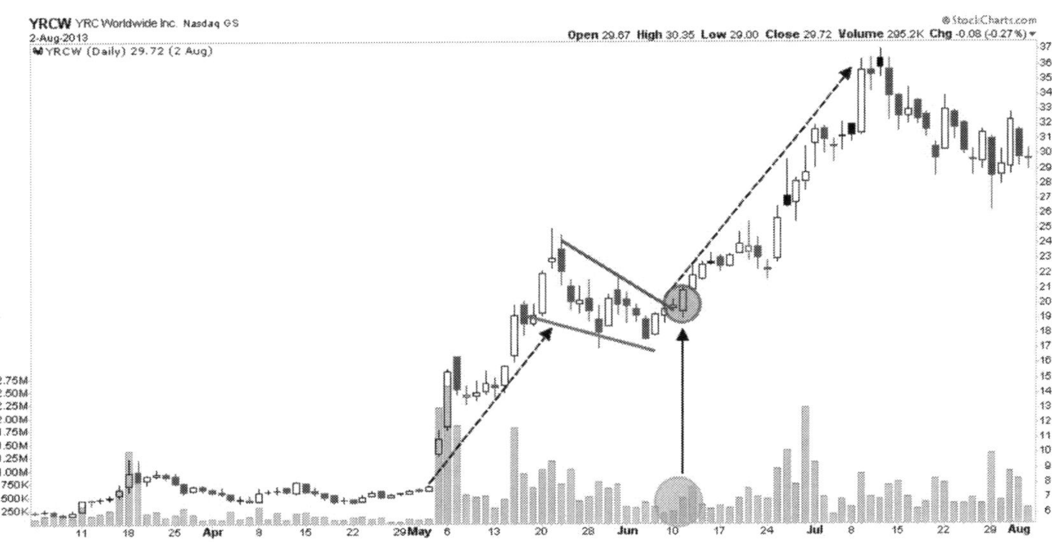

Figure 9.16: YRC Worldwide and a Falling Wedge

The above chart illustrates beautifully that the ascension of the YRC Worldwide is made in two sequences, interspersed by a falling wedge. The latter allows future investors to make a stand. Note the increase in volume on the wedge breakout.

Bearish or Rising Wedge

The rising wedge in a downtrend lays the premises of a new low level. The trading range may take several periods and is characterized by higher highs and higher lows and a decrease of the transaction volumes. Consequently, the second decline begins without the backing of an increase of the volume.

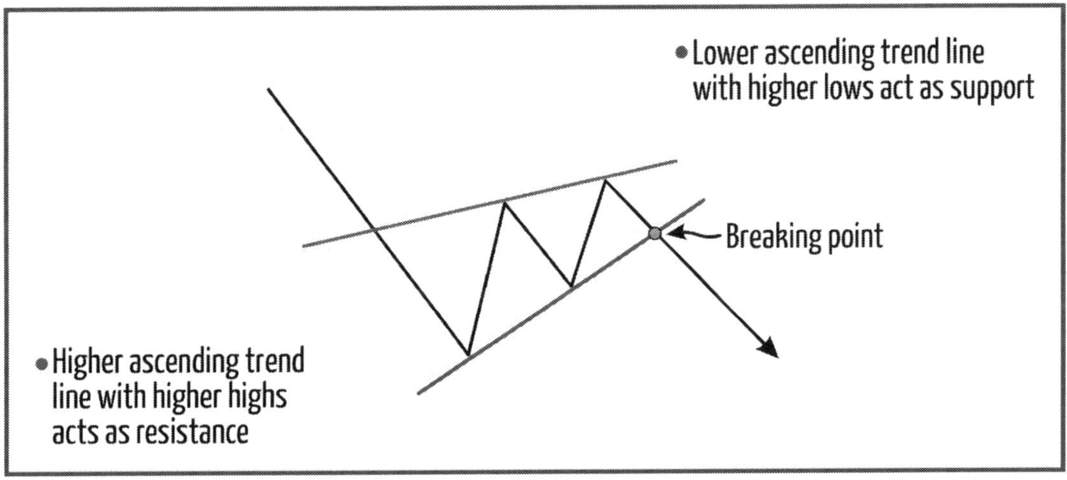

Figure 9.17: Bearish or Rising Wedge. The rising wedge allows anticipating a downward break of a stock. The top and the base of the triangle should be traced by joining at least three candlesticks so that the formation would be recognized as valid. The volume increase on the downward break is not required

The length of the decline before the formation of the triangle is typically used to anticipate the duration of the second decline. The symmetry between the two drops is quite common. The example from 9.18 illustrates the beautiful downtrend, the break, and the second phase of the decline of the stock. Note the lack of the apparent rise of the volume in the fall of the stock.

Figure 9.18: STR Holdings and Rising Wedge

Patterns play an important role in technical analysis. No need for complex mathematical formulas, a glance will suffice. Use patterns with other indicators and you get a powerful combination in your future buying or selling decisions. Despite the fact that the results do not guarantee 100% success, the fact remains that patterns tend to be effective.

Chapter 10 – Reversal Patterns

In technical analysis, a reversal pattern is a chart formation that indicates a market top or a market bottom. A reversal pattern usually occurs at the end of a trend, upward or downward. Investors must change their strategies to take advantage of the new trend to come. We can never repeat enough the importance of drawing some trend lines above and below the candlesticks. It is possible to detect patterns without any calculations. Don't forget that these patterns apply to stock markets, indices and sectors. Reversal patterns are numerous, but we will focus on the most popular. Here is a short list:

- Bump and run reversal bottom
- Bump and run reversal top
- Double bottom
- Double top
- Triple bottom
- Triple top
- Head-and-shoulders bottom
- Head-and-shoulders top
- Rounding bottom
- Parabolic rise

These patterns are easy to identify and can even be spotted by tools available on the web or from your brokerage firm. The reversal patterns often have a higher efficiency than the continuation patterns. It is easier to anticipate the buy or sell signals on these kinds of figures. Be on the lookout, as these patterns could generate important gains. Pay attention to the weekly patterns; potential gains will be greater than the stocks identified on a daily chart.

Bump and Run Reversal Bottom

The bump and run reversal bottom is a pattern that announces an upward trend reversal of a stock or index. It is characterized by a soft-angled decline followed by a more rapid drop in share price. Consequently, the stock will reach an extreme low, consolidate its position and come back in power. We could observe a type of V-shape. The buy signal is confirmed by a rising break of the meeting point between thc first slope and the recent upward line.

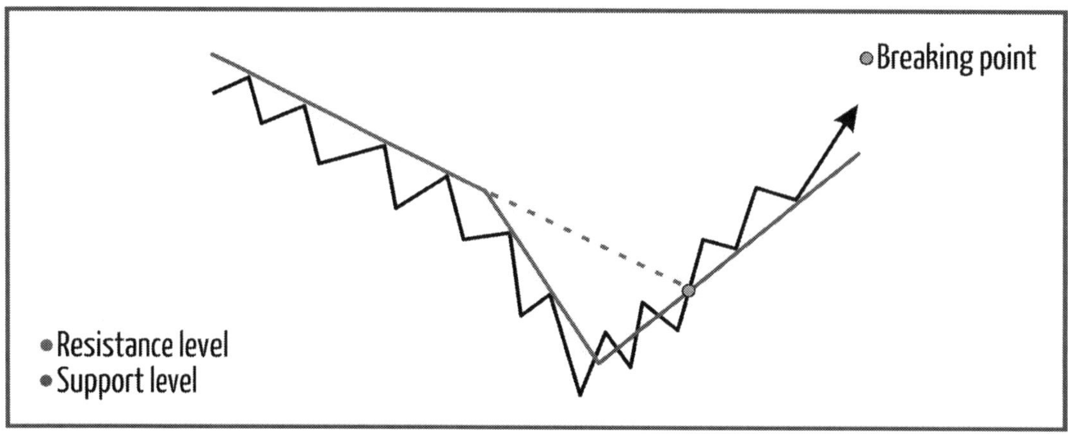

Figure 10.1: The Bump and Run Reversal Bottom is an upward reversal pattern characterized by two types of decline; a moderated one and an accelerated one. It gives the investors all the time necessary to be well positioned. It is, therefore, possible to anticipate an entry point

When the stock accelerates its decline, we could already prepare ourselves to monitor the reversal threshold closely. Consequently, simply wait for the break signal to invest in the stock. This pattern has been recognized by Thomas Bulkowski and was originally named Bump and run formation.

Figure 10.2: James River Coal and a Bump and Run Reversal Bottom

The figure above presents the chart of James River Coal. The bump and run reversal bottom pattern extends over a period of six months. The figure, although complex at first glance, shows the downward spiral of the stock, its agony and its resurrection. Notice the buy signal generated in early May. Investors who spotted this buy signal obtain substantial profits. Backing off the volume on the rise of the stock is unequivocal.

Bump and Run Reversal Top

The bump and run reversal top is a pattern that announces a downward trend reversal of a stock or index. It is characterized by a moderate angle increase, followed by a steeper rise in the share price. Consequently, the stock will reach an extreme summit, consolidate its position and make a downward reversal.

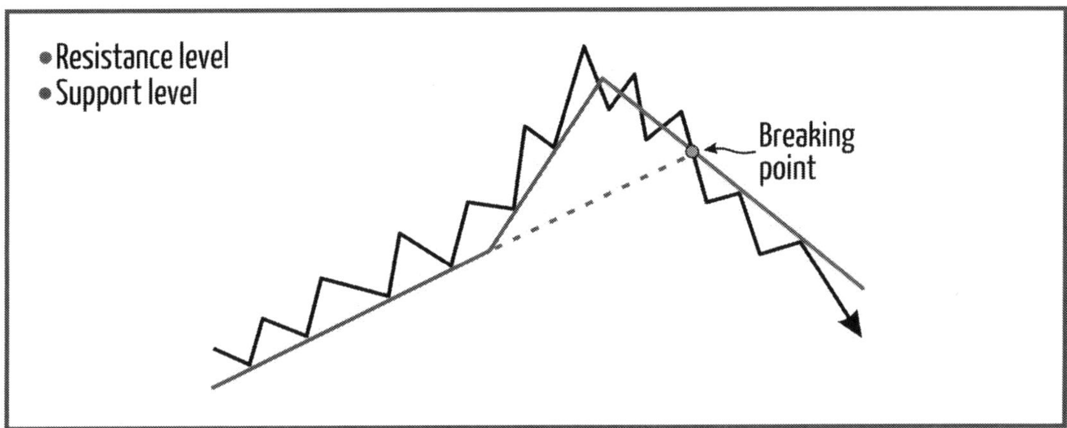

Figure 10.3: Bump and Run Reversal Top. This pattern is characterized by two types of rising: a moderated one and an accelerated one. For the short-selling specialists, this is one of the greatest patterns. We could start preparing ourselves for a rapid descent to compensate for the unrestrained increase that the stock has just been through.

It looks like a reverse pattern of a V-shape. The sell signal is confirmed by the downward break of the meeting point between the first rising slope and the recent bottom line. This configuration often appears when stocks are in an uptrend, and an alarm suddenly leads investors to invest in bulk. The final climb is more pronounced, or even parabolic, and usually announces an imminent collapse.

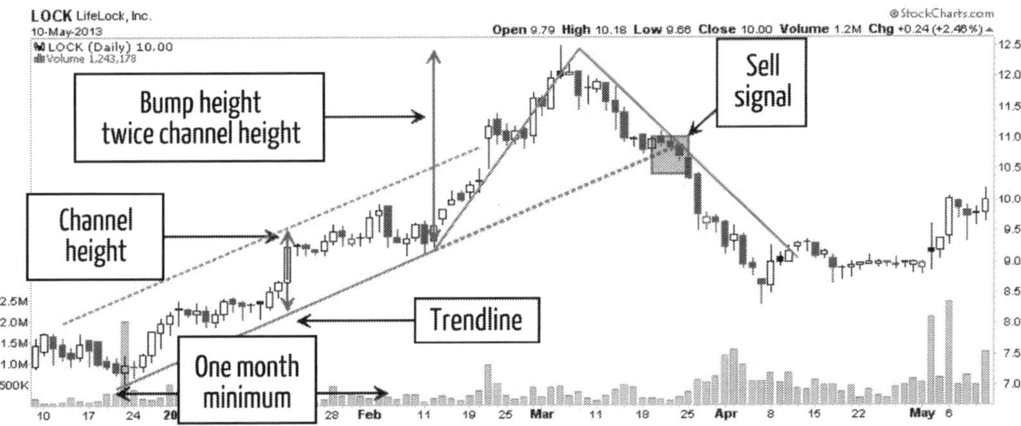

Figure 10.4: LifeLock and a Bump and Run Reversal Top

Double and Triple Bottom

The double bottom is a succession of two peaks of the same amplitude, offering a certain symmetry. This pattern takes the shape of a W. Lower reversal points represent the support area or neckline. Stock price bounces twice on this support and suggests a trend reversal. Bad news related to the stock or industry sector can explain the drop. After a long fall, the price forms a major bottom. Consequently, the stock makes a midterm retrenchment.

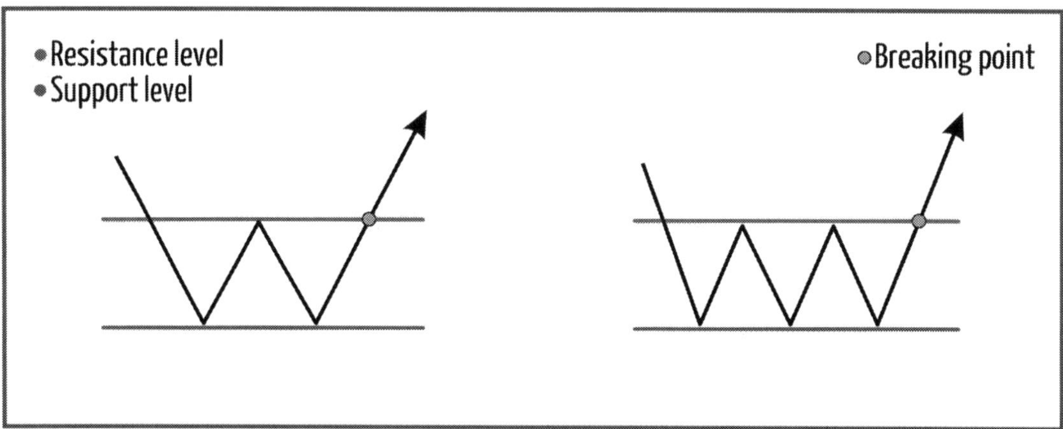

Figure 10.5: Double Bottom. The double bottom is a reversal pattern that occurs after a downtrend and that extends over many periods (50 to 100). The pattern is confirmed by the break of the resistance line on heavy volume. The potential target is determined by adding the height of the W to the resistance line

Support and resistance lines are taking shape. Several investors take advantage to sell, after losing faith in the stock. The share price should fall to the same level as the previous low. After completing the second bottom, the stock goes back up, breaks through the resistance line and follows its growth.

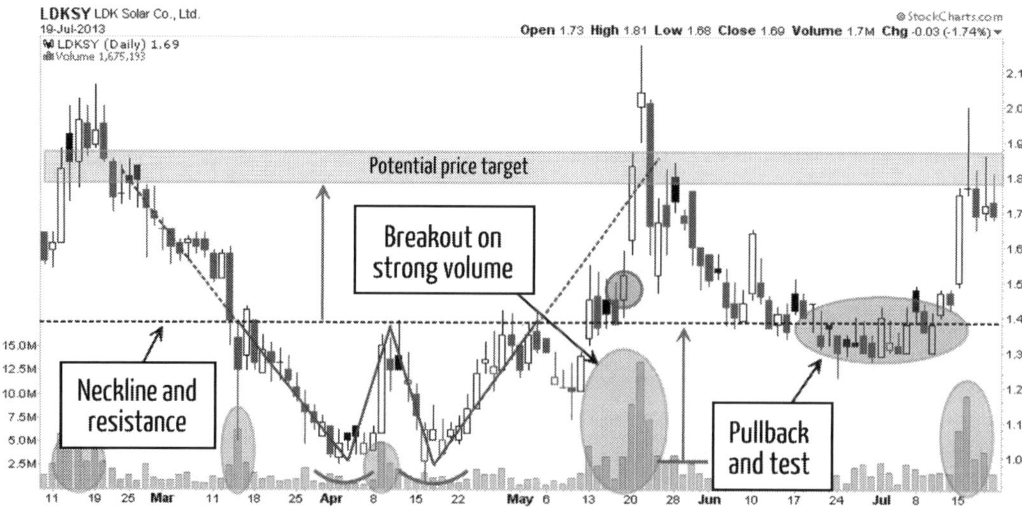

Figure 10.6: LDK Solar and a Double Bottom

The figure 10.6 shows LDK Solar during a double bottom. Notice how the height of W under the neckline is similar to the gap between the neckline and the potential target. Don't hesitate to cash in your profits. Notice how quickly the stock retraced this path at the end of May. In June, the neckline was tested again, and the support was able to resist many attacks by traders. Furthermore, note the volume increase when the stock price reached the resistance, support or the potential target. The triple top is much rarer than the double top but has similar characteristics.

Double and Triple Top

The double top is a downward reversal pattern. This model takes the shape of the letter M. The inability to cross a higher level can be seen, caused by a major resistance area. The pattern shows two peaks, roughly symmetrical with respect to the duration and amplitude. After the first leg of the rise, the investors cash in their profits, and the stock drops in the intermediate zone. It will be followed by a rebound, which will form the support line. A second rise comes up against resistance. There are more sellers than buyers. The trend reversal is taking place.

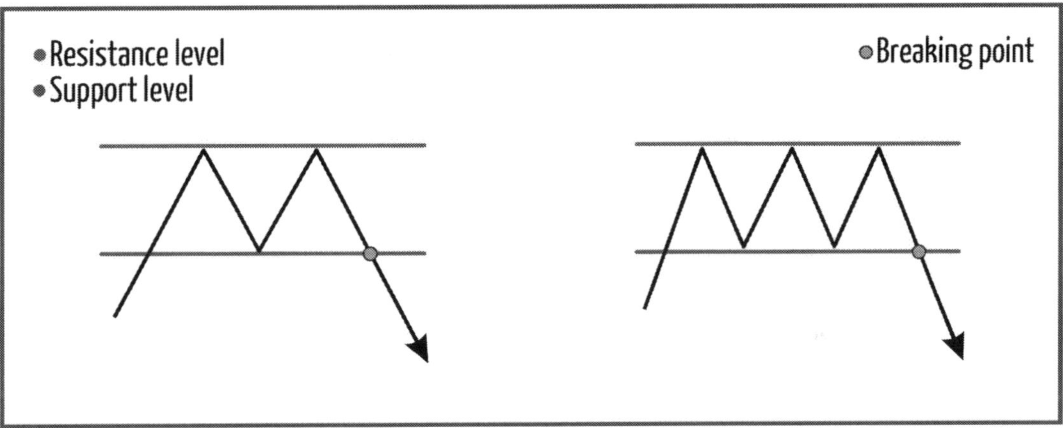

Figure 10.7: The Double Top is a reversal that occurs following an uptrend that spans many periods (50 to 100). The figure is confirmed by the breakdown of the support line. The potential target is determined by subtracting the height of the M from the support line

The stock continues to fall and breaks its support area. A sell signal is given, and the stock pursues its decline. A certain panic arises. The final target of the decline will be equal to twice the amplitude between the resistance and the support zones. Double top patterns are very common in stock charts. They can be recognized in different periods (hours, days, weeks). Pull support and resistance lines in order to anticipate entry and exit points.

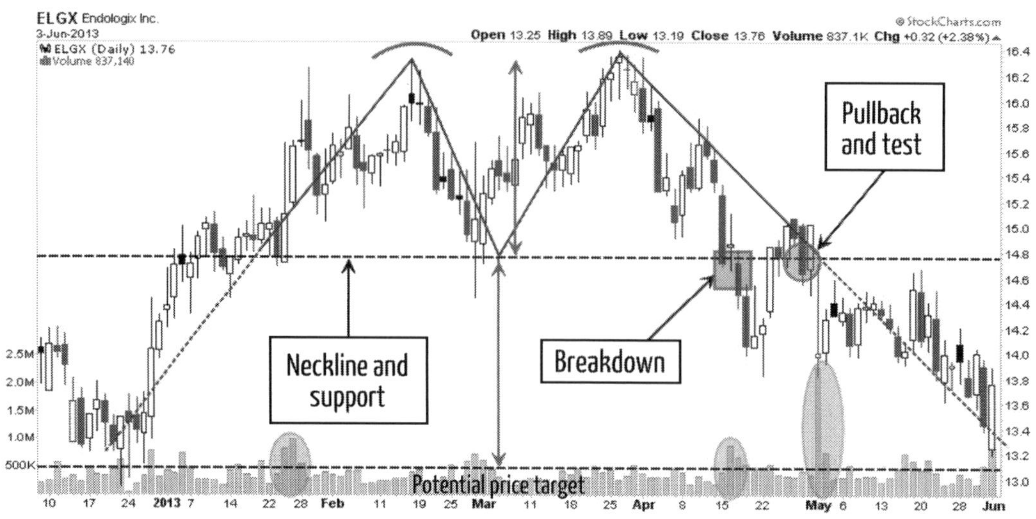

Figure 10.8: Endologix and a Double Top

The figure above shows a perfect double top pattern. The resistance zone at top prevents the stock price from moving forward twice. The first correction will determine the neckline and temporary support. Consequently, the stock price goes back and tests the resistance zone a second time. This configuration strengthens the validity of the pattern because it reflects a lack of buyers. A second correction will occur, and the downward reversal will be validated by the neckline break.

Head-and-Shoulders Bottom

The head-and-shoulders bottom is a pattern found quite often, and it's valued by many chartists. This pattern is a trend reversal made through three successive bottoms. Head-and-shoulders bottom resembles the upper body of a man but reversed at 180 degrees. This pattern confirms an upward trend on the neckline break. It's particularly efficient in a weekly format, which is excellent for long-term investors.

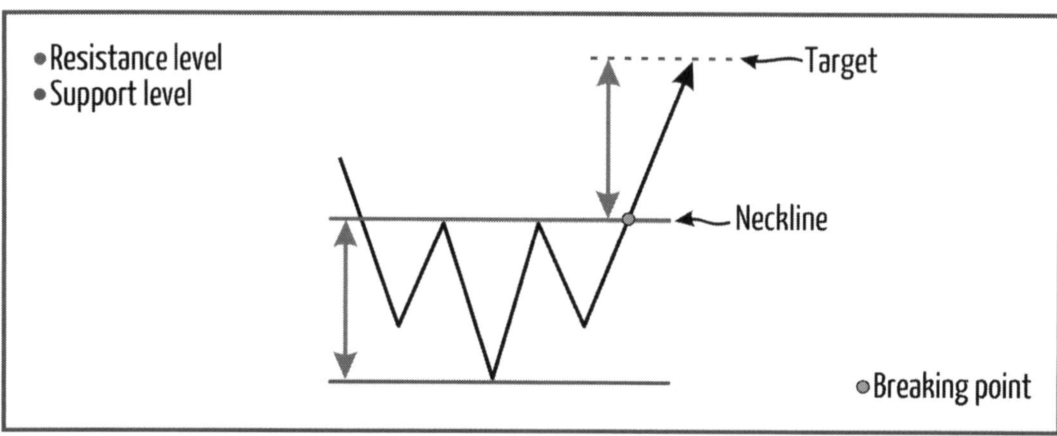

Figure 10.9: The Head-and-Shoulders Bottom pattern is one of the most efficient trend reversal patterns. The neckline is tested three times and breaks under the pressure from buyers.

Figure 10.10: Yingli Green Holding and a Head-and-Shoulders Bottom

The figure above illustrates the head-and-shoulders bottom pattern for Yingli Green. The peaks reached between the different bottoms also build the neckline and the resistance. The neckline is not necessarily horizontal. The validity of this model is based on the strength of the neckline breakout. The breaking volume is the key factor to monitor. A break without a volume increase does not guarantee success.

Head-and-Shoulders Top

The head-and-shoulders top is the inverse figure of the head-and-shoulders bottom. Its accuracy is quite disconcerting. This pattern suggests a reversal of the downward trend and resembles the top of a human body: head, shoulders, and torso.

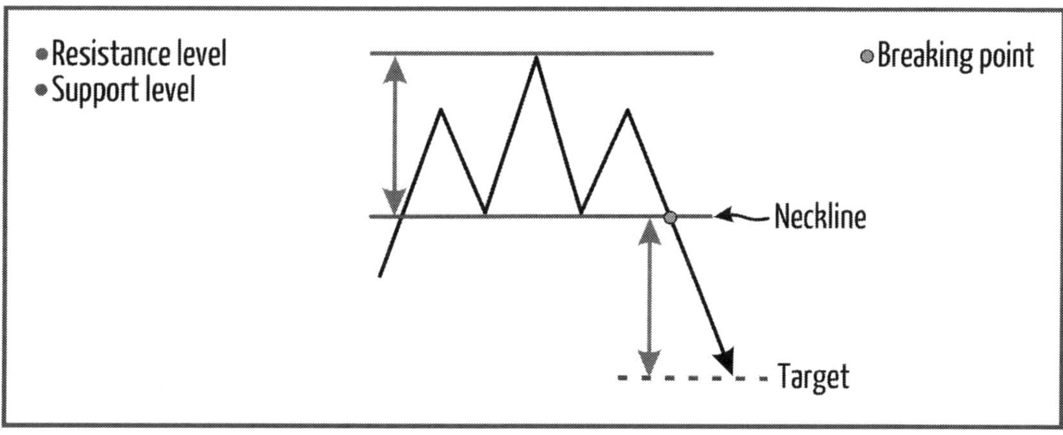

Figure 10.11: The Head-and-Shoulders Top is a trend reversal pattern formed by three peaks. We can already anticipate the pattern during the head formation. An increase in volume is present during the creation of each peak. The neckline is tested three times.

The pattern takes shape in five steps:

Step 1

The left shoulder is formed by the first peak, followed by a decline that helps generate the neckline.

Step 2

The head is represented by a higher peak, followed by a decline that comes to rely on the neckline.

Step 3

The right shoulder is formed by the last peak. Give some importance to the symmetry of the shoulders, both in height and width. Some purists require a perfect symmetry. This requirement ensures that this pattern would be virtually non-existent and so useless in terms of learning.

Step 4

Always look out for a false breaking signal. It occurs when a candlestick closes below the neckline.

Step 5

In many cases, the height of the drop following the neckline break should be equivalent to the distance between the head and the neckline.

Figure 10.12: Walter Energy and a Head-and-Shoulders Top

The figure above shows the potential target of Walter Energy stock. Note the symmetry of the length of the model. The figure took almost three years to build. The gap between the head and the neckline is $80 ($140-$60). To establish the potential target, simply subtract the difference of $80 from the neckline value. In this case, we have a potential target of $20 under zero ($60 minus $80). This pattern is appreciated by the short-sale specialists because the breaking of the neckline marks the absence of the support, mainly caused by the long-term pattern. Many buyers of 2008–2009 left the ship a long time ago.

Rounding Bottom

The rounding bottom is characterized by periodic low-volume transactions and small price differentials. To be valid, this pattern must extend a minimum of 20–40 periods. Even if it seems awfully difficult to follow, the rounding bottom pattern is one of the most explosive patterns.

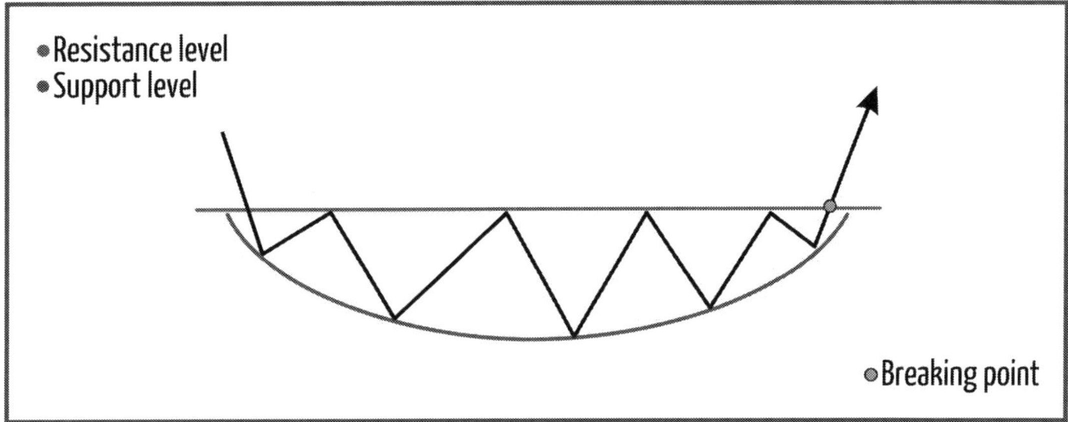

Figure 10.13: Rounding Bottom pattern. Are you tired of following a stock whose price goes through a short amplitude corridor? This model can lead to fabulous profits.

The stocks that have this type of pattern require investors who have a dose of extreme patience. We are in a period of accumulation; buyers dominate the market. Generally speaking, the longer the accumulation, the stronger the breakout will be once it occurs. There's no need to use mobile averages or other indicators; simply locate the resistance level and draw a line. Check the progress of each stock on a daily basis. Just wait for the break of the resistance line to take action.

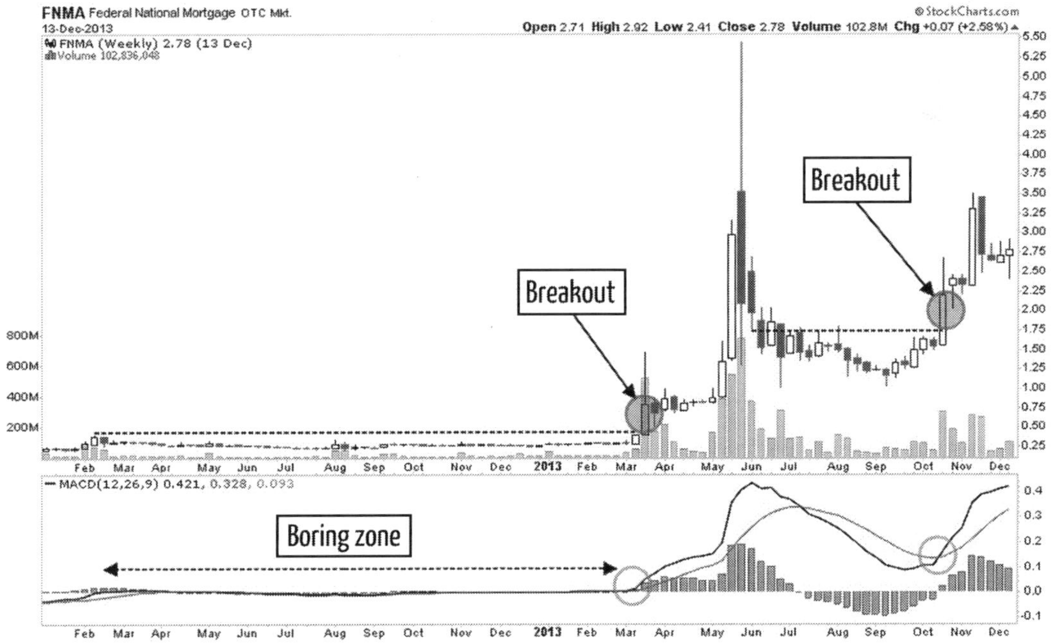

Figure 10.14: Federal National Mortgage and a Rounding Bottom

The figure 10.14 shows two rounding bottoms, the first being two times longer than the second. Your input is simple. Draw a horizontal line representing the resistance and wait for the stock to break that line. The breakout of the resistance line has to be made on high volumes, as in every upward scenario. Notice the strong volume during the first breakout.

The scenario is repeated again in 2013. The accumulation period was shorter because the investors who missed the first bottom smelled a good deal and started accumulating stock in order to be ready for the second race. MACD was added, and it helps in decision-making. It clearly shows when to take action. When you see stocks in a consolidation period such as this one, you know that you have to place them on a watchlist in order to be ready for any eventuality.

The Parabolic Rise

As its name suggests, this figure illustrates the meteoric increase of a stock in a parabolic form. This pattern is caused by a high level of speculation. When you believe that the rise is complete, the acceleration of the increase continues even more beautifully. This type of movement valued by day traders is difficult to manage for all investors.

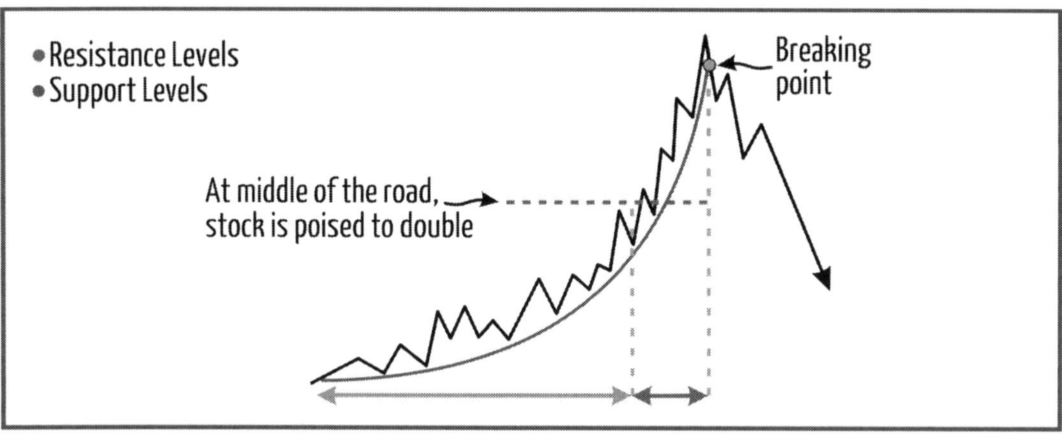

Figure 10.15: Parabolic Rise. This pattern is similar to an arc of which the source is located on the horizontal axis, and the end is based on the vertical axis. This model targets more often experienced traders who use short selling. The strategy is to wait for the downward break of the curve and sell short. The descent is usually much faster than the rising.

This model presents many traps, and it is often connected to stocks with a high level of volatility. It is difficult to anticipate the exit point. Tracking this pattern is delayed. It can be identified when it is at halfway. At this point, it is possible to draw an arc as a guide to determine the future breakout.

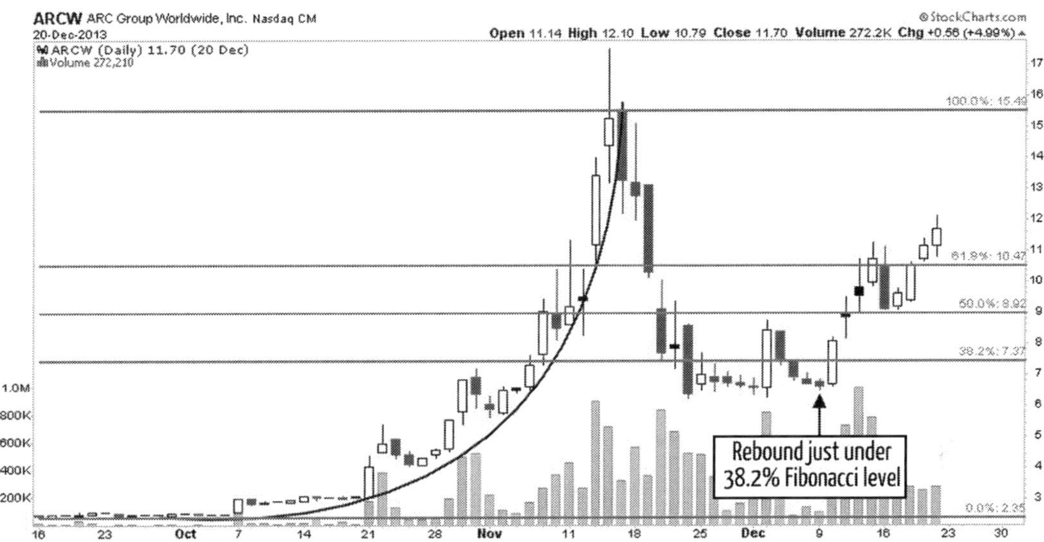

Figure 10.16: ARC Wireless Solutions and a Parabolic Rise

The chart above shows an exponential surge for Arc Wireless Solutions. In less than two months, the stock passed from \$1 to \$16. Completely amazing, folks! The stock seems to be supported by the arc traced on the base of the candlesticks. The downward break of the drawing sends out a sell signal. The professionals are happy seeing this pattern and are positioning themselves to short sell and cash fabulous profits.

Chapter 11 – Candlesticks Patterns

As we saw in **Chapter 1**, the Japanese candlesticks show in detail the price of a share for one period (minute, hour, day, week). Furthermore, as every technical indicator does, the candlesticks can generate trend reversal models or patterns useful for analyzing stocks. When the time comes to make an investment decision, the candlesticks are not enough. Do not see the candlesticks as a different way to analyze charts. You should rather see the candlesticks as a complement to the technical analysis. The candlesticks have to be combined with other indicators seen in previous chapters to maximize your investment decisions.

Use the candlesticks and its many configurations. Develop a routine of drawing your support and resistance lines, corridors, trend, triangles or other figures seen before. For example, during a double bottom pattern, pay attention to the presence of a candlestick that may announce an upward trend reversal. Closely monitor the support and resistance line breaks. The length of a candlestick measures the amplitude of the market's indecision.

Watch suits of candlesticks that have the same color. They announce a powerful signal of trend continuation. The combination of Japanese candlesticks and traditional technical analysis is the best way to consider all the strengths and weaknesses found in stocks. As this book is addressed to beginners, we will focus on the most significant configurations. For those who want to perfect their knowledge, numerous works have already been written on this subject. Know that there are nearly one hundred different figures. The use of these models must be combined with your favorite indicators in order to maximize your analysis. As technical indicators, the candlesticks do not allow you to predict the future.

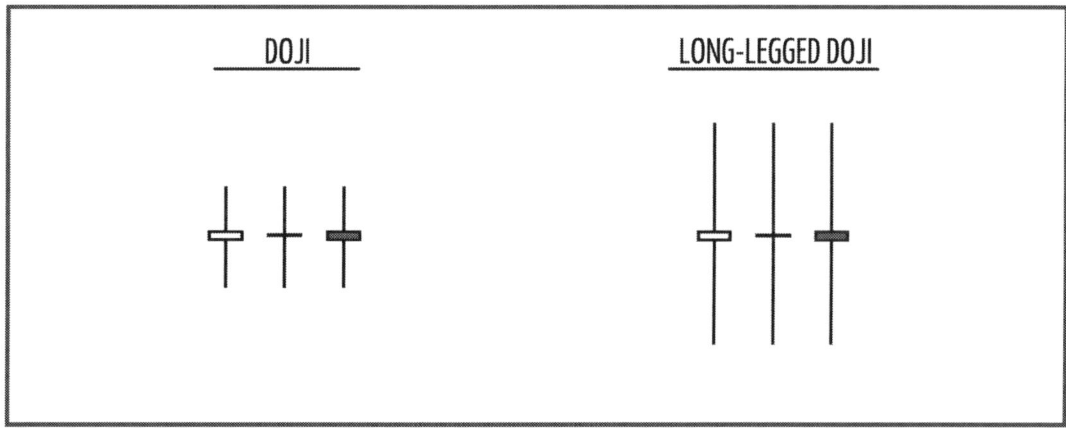

Figure 11.1: Doji and Long-Legged doji. Pattern type: neutral. This candlestick presents average or long shades that indicate a neutral trend for the period. It marks a pause and could be the beginning of a new trend. If it reaches support or resistance level, there is a good chance for a trend reversal.

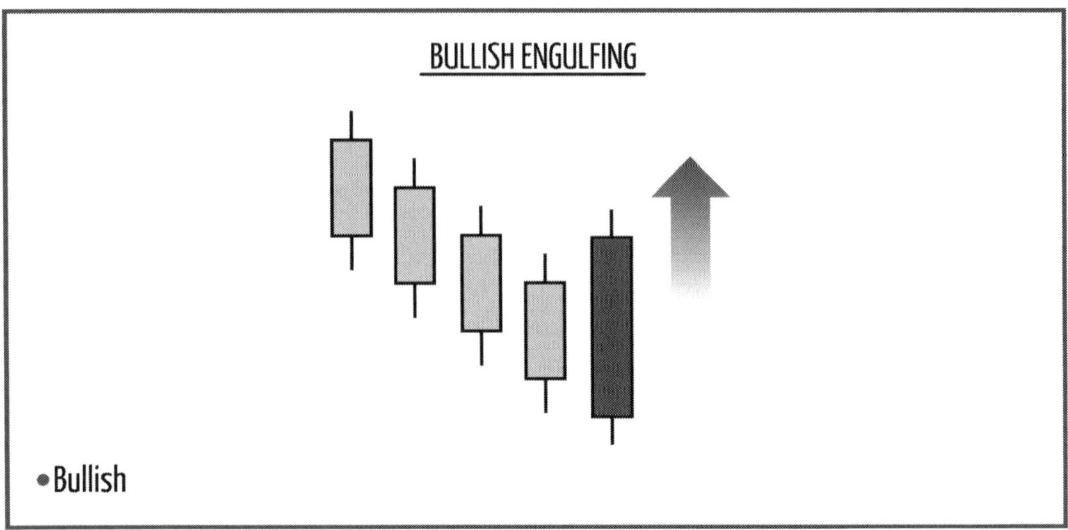

Figure 11.2: Bullish Engulfing. Pattern type: bullish. The bullish engulfing structure is an efficient reversal pattern. It begins below the previous downward red/black candlestick and ends its race above the same candlestick. There comes the engulfing pattern expression. The longer the candlestick is, the more significant the signal will be.

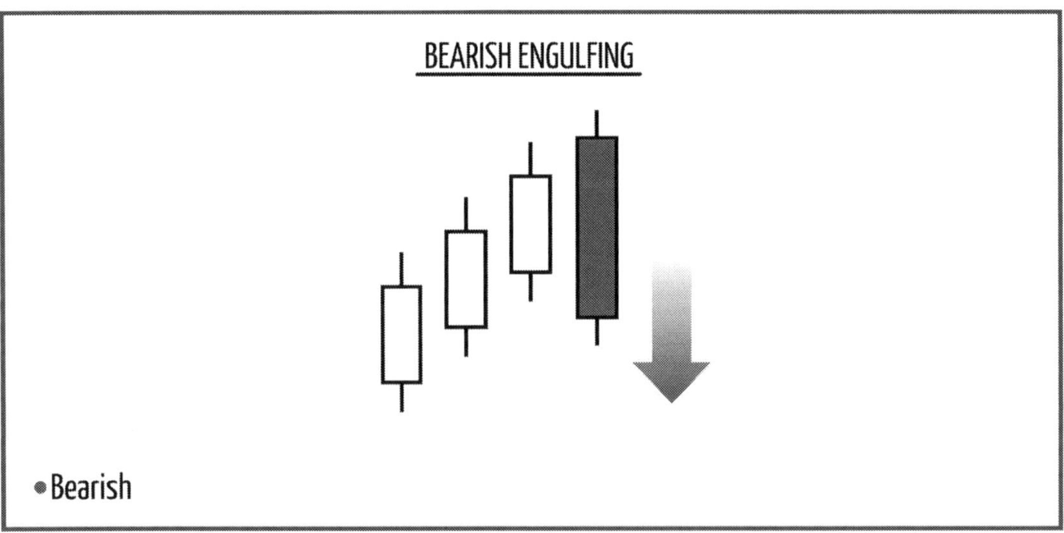

Figure 11.3: Bearish Engulfing. Pattern type: bearish. The bearish engulfing structure is a downtrend reversal pattern. Note that the downward engulfing must start above the previous upward white/green candlestick and finish its race under the same candlestick. The longer the candlestick is, the more significant the signal will be.

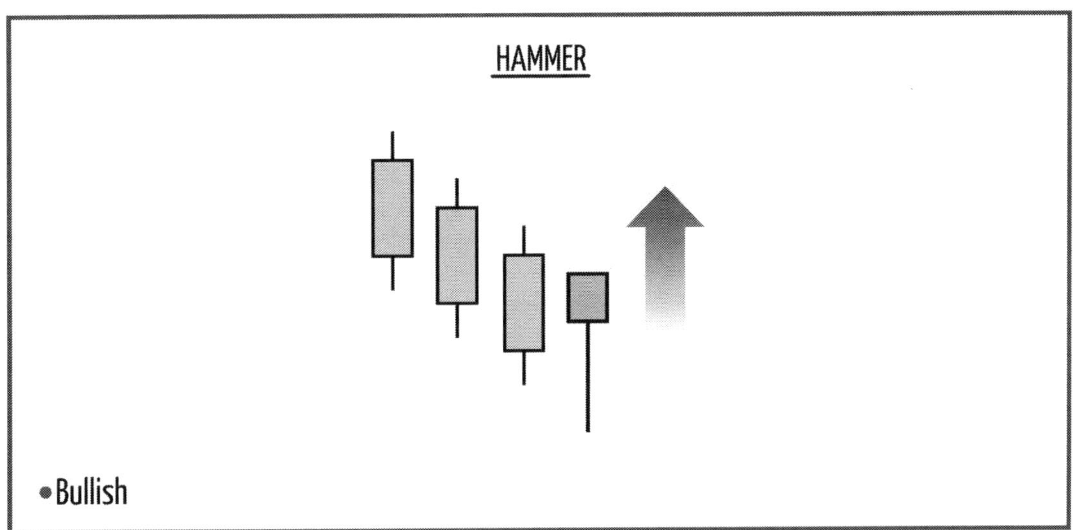

Figure 11.4: Hammer. Pattern type: bullish. The hammer is an upward trend reversal pattern. The hammer knocks out the bottom. The elongated shadow indicates that the stock price has gone through a big selling pressure, but the session ended in strength and a positive way.

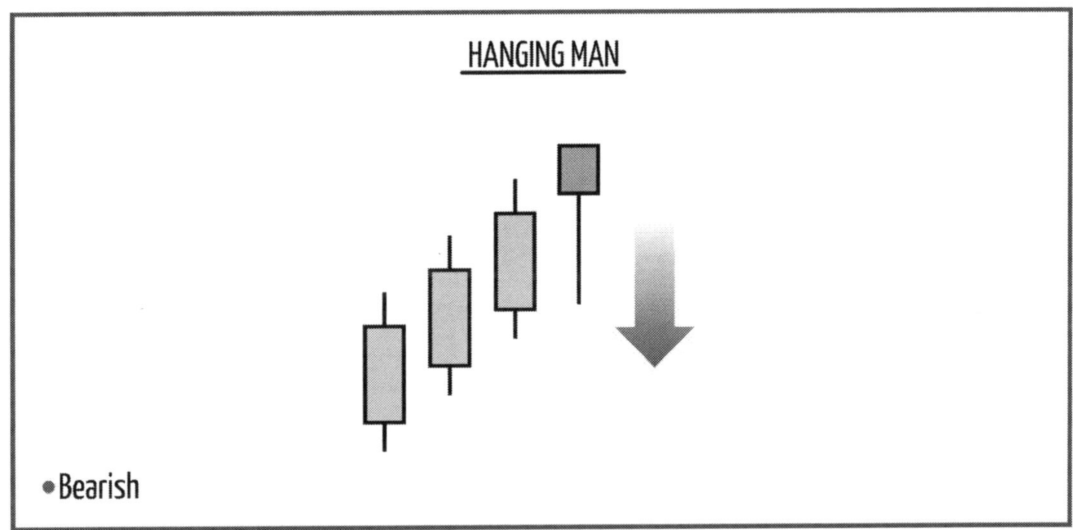

Figure 11.5: Hanging Man. Pattern type: bearish. The hanging man appears after an uptrend. The body of the candlestick should be small and preferably red (negative). The longer the downward shadow is, the stronger the reversal movement will be. The elongated shadow indicates that the stock price has gone through a significant selling pressure.

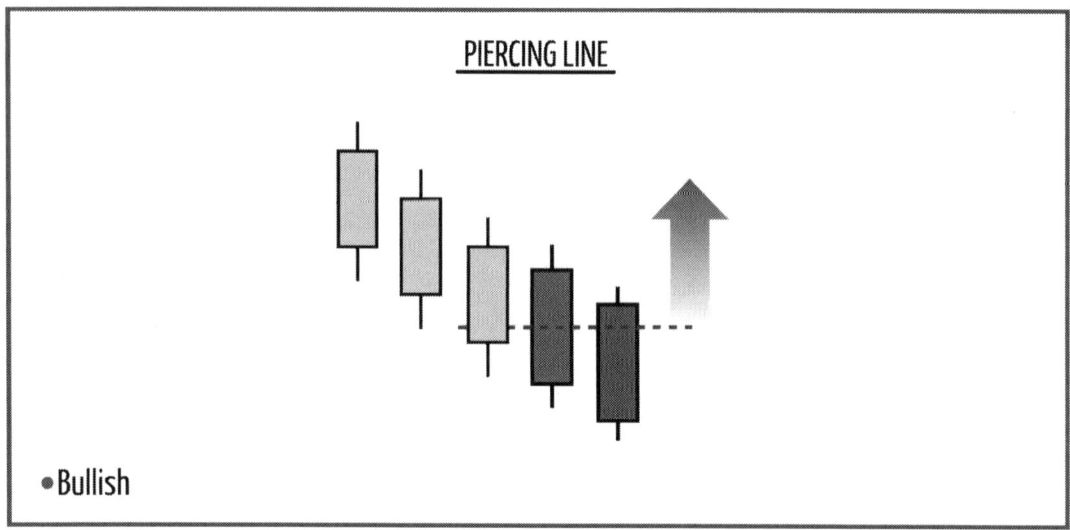

Figure 11.6: Piercing Line. Pattern type: bullish. The piercing line appears after a downtrend. It is a reversal pattern we find in the market's lows. You see a first red/black (negative) candlestick followed by a white/green (positive) candlestick that opens lower and manages to close above the middle of the previous red/black candlestick.

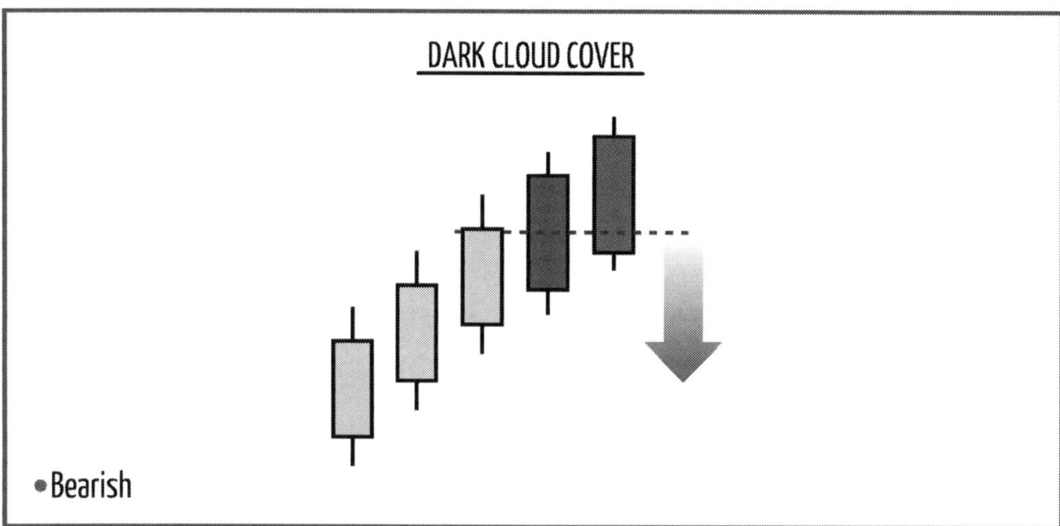

Figure 11.7: Dark Cloud Cover. Pattern type: bearish. The dark cloud cover appears following a bullish trend. This is a reversal pattern we find in the market's highs. There is a first white/green (positive) candlestick, followed by a red/black (negative) candlestick that opens up higher and manages to close below the middle of the previous white/green candlestick.

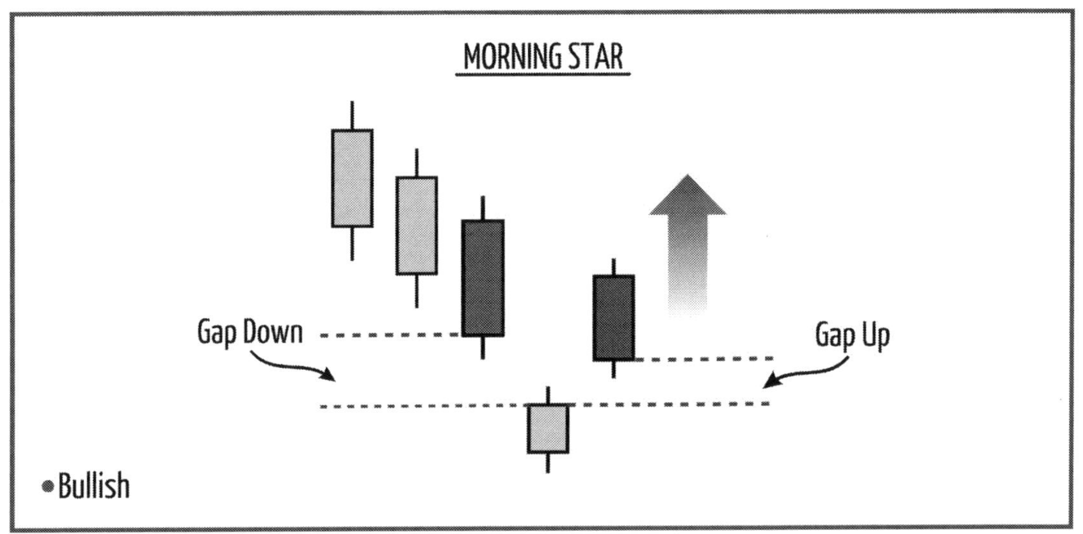

Figure 11.8: Morning Star. Pattern type: bullish. The morning star is symbolized by a doji or a candlestick with a small body (upward or downward) placed in a downtrend. We have to wait for the next upward candlestick to confirm the upward reversal. It is a reversal signal without great conviction.

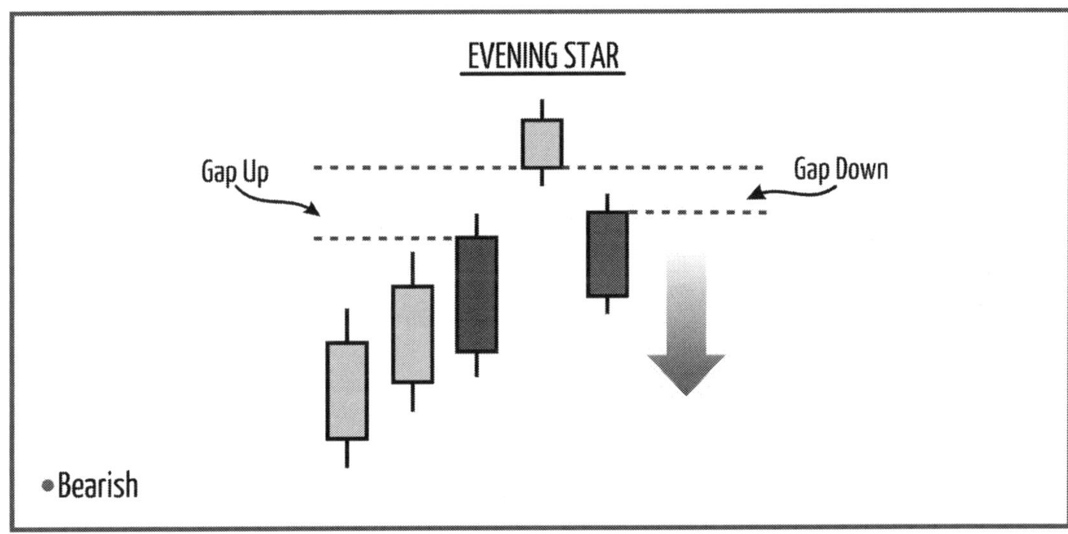

Figure 11.9: Evening Star. Pattern type: bearish. The evening star is represented by a doji or a candlestick with a small body (upward or downward), which is located in an uptrend. The following bearish candlestick confirms the downward reversal. It is a sign of a reversal without great conviction.

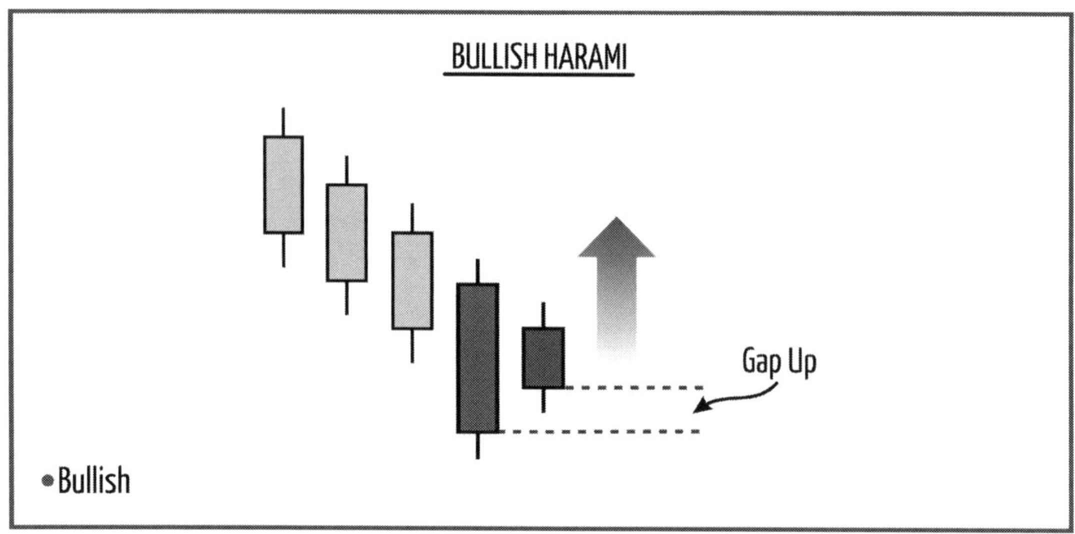

Figure 11.10: Bullish Harami. Pattern type: bullish. The small bullish candlestick (white/green) begins the session with an upward gap. This candlestick is encompassed by the previous bearish (red/black) candlestick. The upward turn is confirmed if the next candlestick is up.

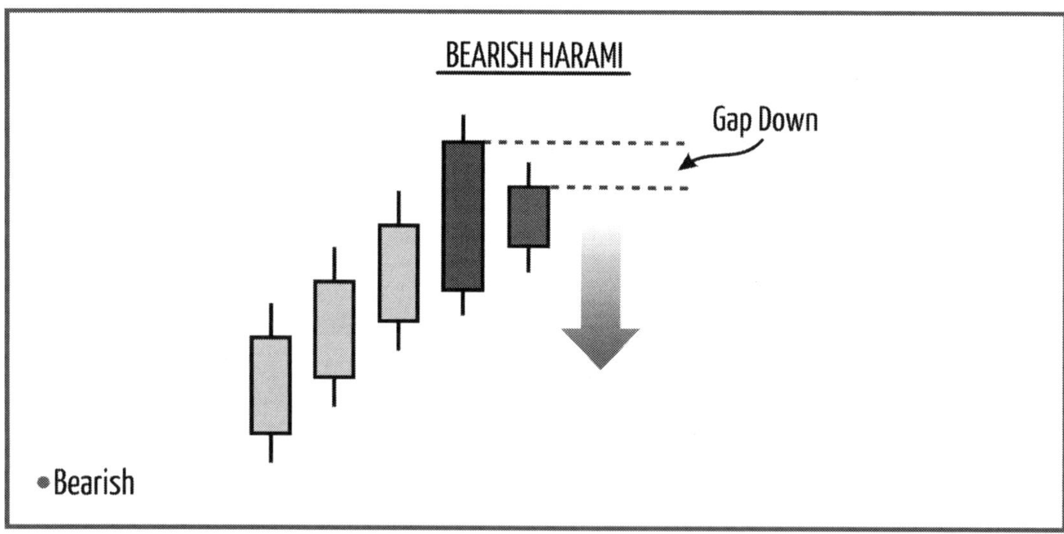

Figure 11.11: Bearish Harami. Pattern type: bearish. The small bearish candlestick (red/black) begins the session with a downward gap. It is encompassed by the previous bullish (white/green) candlestick. The downturn reversal has to be confirmed by another downward candlestick.

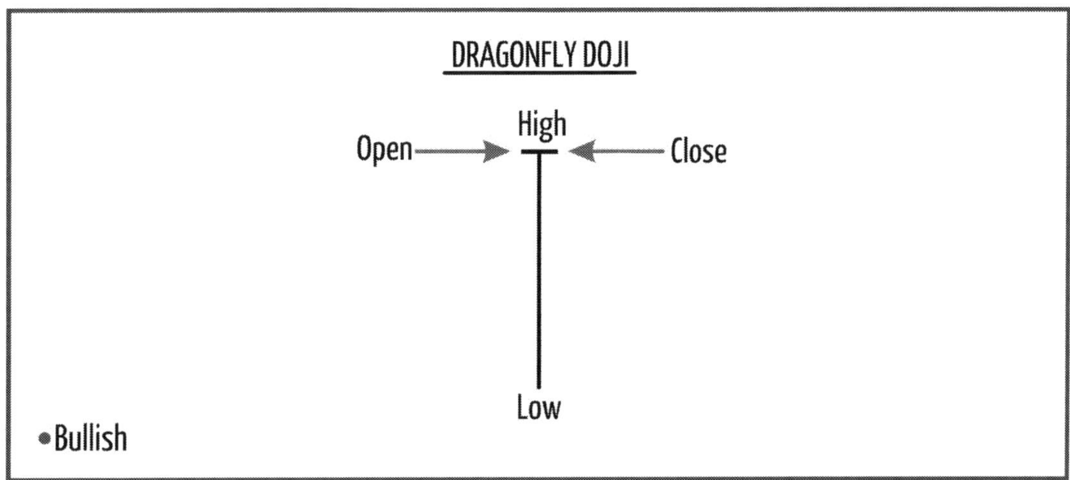

Figure 11.12: Dragonfly Doji. Pattern type: bullish. This candlestick looks like the hammer and is the perfect candlestick in a bull market. Following the opening, a significant decrease occurred, but the market reversed. This allowed the stock to come back to its starting point. The longer the shade, the stronger the impact.

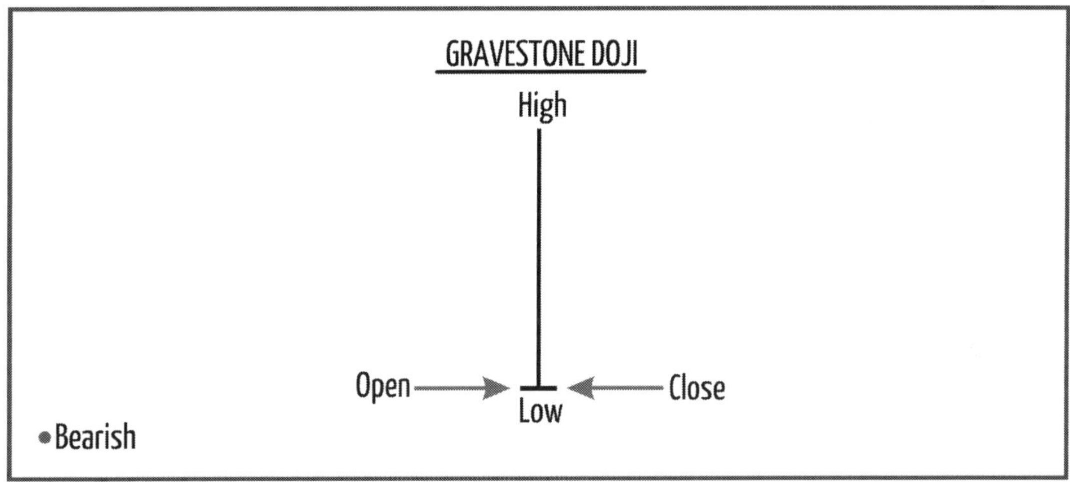

Figure 11.13: Gravestone Doji. Pattern type: bearish. This candlestick looks like an inverse hammer and represents the candlestick that nobody wants to see when invested in a bull market. This candlestick is formed when the opening and closing price are equal and represents the low of the day. The long upper shadow suggests that the buying pressure of the day has been blocked by the sellers. It could be a major reversal.

Japanese candlesticks provide many configurations. Several financial tools provide the possibility to search for your favorite patterns. Your brokerage firm might offer such tools. Combine the candlestick patterns with the technical indicators, and your analysis will be more precise. Learn how to spot these basic patterns quickly.

Chapter 12 – Avoid the Traps

Technical analysis is a system whose efficiency is recognized. However, don't believe that this efficiency can reach 100 percent, especially since investors must cope with high-frequency trading. This trading mode is executed by specialized companies that have a huge advantage over small investors. The best traders in the world have an efficiency rate of 80 to 90%. So, sooner or later, you will face an unexpected reversal. The idea of this chapter is to learn from your mistakes and avoid them in the future. There are many errors, most of them caused by our emotions, that can gradually consume our good judgment and our capital.

Fibonacci Retracement

The Fibonacci retracement is a useful tool to extrapolate the amplitude of some movements. Retracements only serve to give potential targets. The principle is simple: at the end of a bull cycle with nice amplitude, you have to foresee the possibility of a pullback of 38.2%. Pay attention; market forces can ensure a stock to fall by 50% or even 62.8%. Here is the Fibonacci sequence presented in Chapter 5:

1, 1, 2, 3, 5, 8, 13, 21, 34, 55, 89, 144, 233, . . .

The tool shows the 38.2%, 50% and 61.8% retracements. The first ratio is calculated by dividing whichever number of the sequence by the second number that follows it. For example, 8/21 means 38.09% and 13/34 results 38.23%. The third ratio of 61.8% is calculated by dividing any number of the sequence by the first following number. For example, 8/13 results in 61.54% and 13/21 results in 61.90%. Not that some financial providers do not offer the Fibonacci retracement.

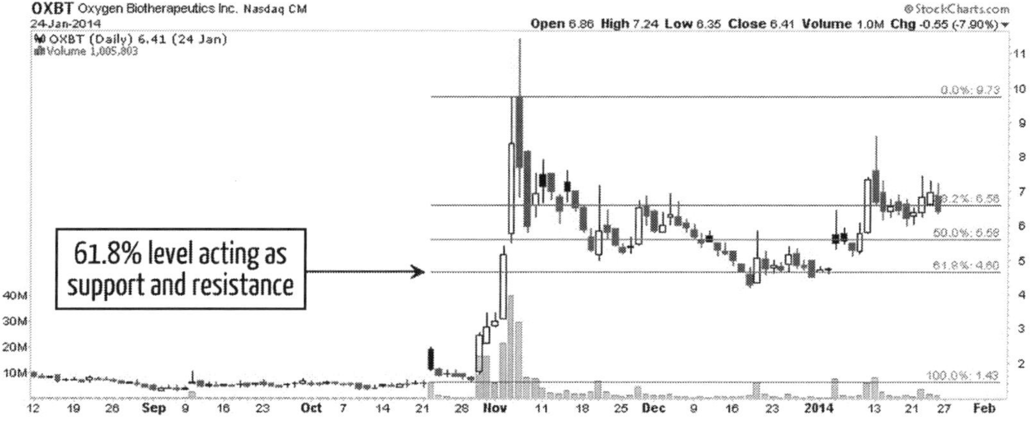

Figure 12.1: Oxygen Biotherapeutics and the Fibonacci retracement

The figure 12.1 shows the pullback of Oxygen Biotherapeutics shares after having reached a new top in early November. The decline has fully stopped at 61.8%, to bounce off the 50% level. However, don't believe that these levels act as magnets. Many investors watch these levels and act at the same time. The Fibonacci retracement help set targets and rebounds. Use this tool for each bullish or bearish cycle; it will be helpful in your projections.

Fake Head-and-Shoulders

Take time to analyze your stocks by including as many tools as possible in order to highlight signs of reversals or simply to watch for fake signals. Do not only draw trend lines for the stock price but also for indicators and volumes. Despite the potential power of a figure that emerges, a fake signal could be generated.

Figure 12.2: Renren and a false Head-and-Shoulders Bottom

The Renren stock featured a head-and-shoulders bottom pattern, merely a bit deformed, which didn't stop it from making a break higher than 10%. Two elements emerge from this chart. Firstly, the volume decrease since mid-May announced the failure of the neckline break. Secondly, the absence of a significant increase in volume on the breakout has stopped its momentum and has made it plunge more than 20% during June. A downward volume during a price increase cannot last for a long time. You don't need many indicators to analyze a figure; simple trend lines may be sufficient in many cases.

No Trend at All

A chart without trend with weak volume are lobster traps for the beginners. Unless you have the scoop of the century, avoid this kind of share at all costs. Quite often, these securities are registered in the secondary market, have some financial problems or do not respect the rules prescribed by the stock markets. We can count many 'pump-and-dump' websites that use these penny stocks and artificially place overbids on stocks that are worthless. Due to their low volume of transactions, the data connected to various indicators is of poor quality. You cannot have a reliable indicator. Avoid the gurus who make recommendations based on these kinds of stocks. It is nothing more than a lottery in which you have very little chance of winning.

Figure 12.3: Atlanticus Holdings—A messy chart

You should avoid stocks that have a chart similar to the one of Atlanticus Holdings. Its transaction average is less than 5,000 per day. Some days, there is no trading at all. Avoid traps that are presented to you and protect your assets from relevant variations.

Adjust Your Moving Averages

One day, you will surely have the chance to see one of your stocks have an exponential boost in a few days. The most difficult thing for you would be to find the best-selling point. To give you a little help, reduce moving averages that you commonly use. The base junction created by two moving averages will launch a sell signal more quickly.

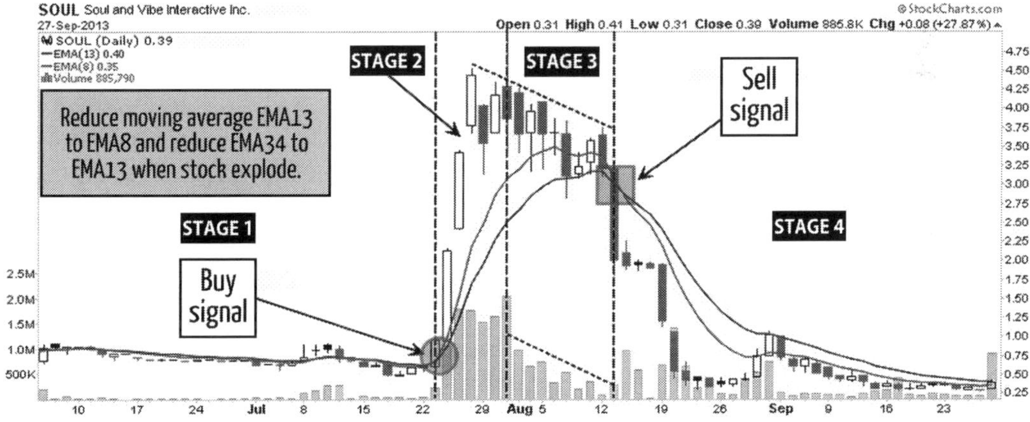

Figure 12.4: Soul and Vibe Interactive and the moving averages

Soul and Vibe Interactive presents the four stages of a stock in a daily format. As the rise was dazzling, you must use a lower moving average, such as an EMA8 combined with an EMA13, to detect the sell signal. A significant drop in volume in stage 3 and the impossibility to stop its downward trend were sufficient to allow the stock to fall more than 30% in a single day. Notice the panic in the volume when crossing the moving averages.

Risky Symmetrical Triangle

The symmetrical triangle is a figure made of two lines opposed, with almost the same slope and whose meeting is manifested by a fall or a substantial increase. Unlike ascending or descending triangle, the symmetrical triangle announces a triangular indecision. It is difficult to anticipate the type of break for this model. It was not until the very end to see the direction of the share price.

Figure 12.5: TCF Financial Corp and a symmetrical triangle

Symmetrical triangles are dangerous because it is difficult to foresee the direction that the stock might take. TCF Financial Corp has been in an uptrend since January. The stock simulated a downward break at the exit of the triangle immediately to take off to a new high. See how the volume increases in July. Volume puts upward pressure on the stock.

Do not waste time trying to anticipate the direction of the breakout for a symmetrical triangle. Before taking any action, wait until a real upside breakout. Thanks to the MACD indicator that shows a strong buy signal a few days later. Always use additional indicators before making an investment decision.

Another Risky Symmetrical Triangle

Here is another example of a symmetrical triangle. The Investors Real Estate Trust has been in an uptrend since January. The symmetrical triangle spans 40 days. Everything led to believe that the stock was pausing before continuing its climb. Without the help of another indicator, it will be necessary to wait for the breakout to take place. The stock hit the highest bar of the triangle in late May and then broke its support.

Figure 12.6: Investors Real Estate Trust and a symmetrical triangle

Before considering a trade, you'll have to be patient and wait for a clear signal to buy or sell the stock. Nothing in the volume level provides an indication this stock will decline for a month. In addition, we have seen previously that the volume had less importance in a breakdown than during a breakout. If you used an EMA34, you would have gotten a sell signal just to the right side of the red square.

Super Rocket Stock

Quite often, some stocks have uncommon increases. Figure 12.7 presents the increase of Cleantech Solutions International, which more than doubled in late May. Unless you're riveted to your screen, forget this type of pattern. Notice the amazing volume compared to the volume of the other days. By chance, if you were positioned before that unthinkable growth, we hope you monitored your stock closely to collect wonderful profits.

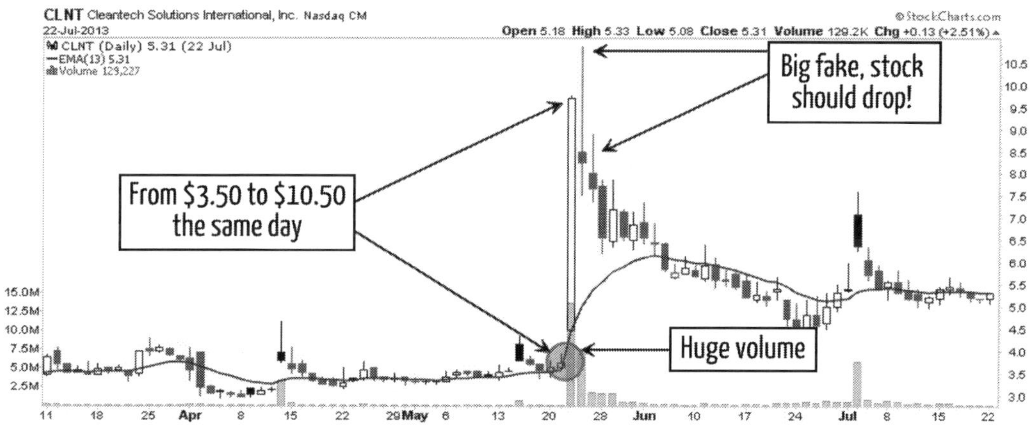

Figure 12.7: Cleantech and a Super Rocket pattern

Nearly 15 million shares were traded in a single day, almost 100 times the average volume of the previous days. Social networks contribute greatly to the acceleration of transactions. Good news spreads like wildfire. The pros accumulate solid gains. The next day, they are ready for a short sale. Several pump-and-dump websites lure newbies with the promise of the following increase, but the fall suddenly happens. Many new traders enter this kind of situation and are royally devoured by the pros.

Long Candles & Long Shadows

New traders enter the market with a certain naivety. They hope for big gains, but the reality is different. To clear their losses, these traders hope to find a guru that will grow their assets. When a guru recommends you invest in a stock similar to figure 12.8, run for your life! These stocks are traps that you must avoid at all costs.

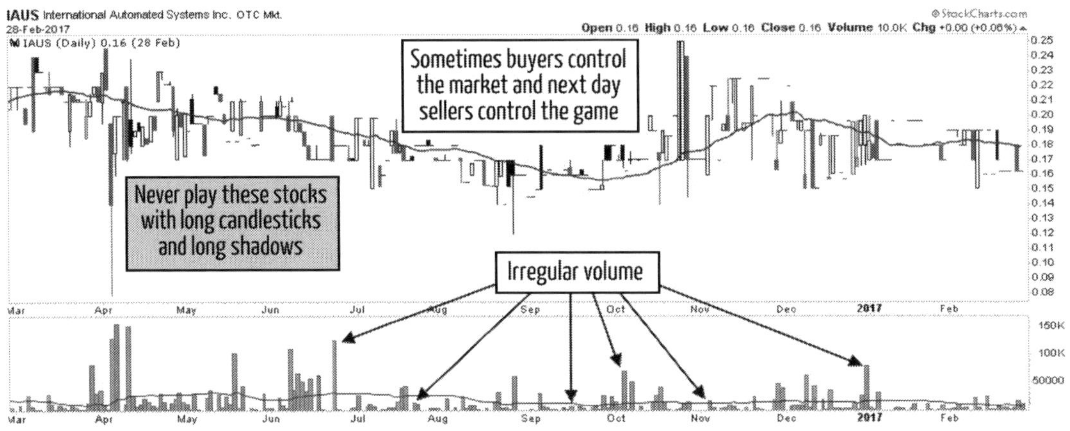

Figure 12.8: International Automated Systems & long candles

The chart of International Automated Systems is one of the most beautiful traps a new investor could invest in. This stock does not show any particular trend. The candlesticks seem disordered, as if someone has tampered with the data. The long shadows of the candlesticks confirm unusual price gaps for most of the trading days.

In fact, there are days when buyers dominate, and the next day, suddenly, the sellers are back in charge. It is impossible to find a bullish or bearish pattern that would allow investing. Buyers and sellers cannot agree on a precise trend to give to the stock. The weak volume of transactions brings gaps between offer and demand. This type of distortion should be avoided. These charts often apply to companies with a small stock market capitalization. Avoid this kind of stock; there are hundreds of stocks that offer much more potential.

Chapter 13 – Trading Psychology

The pressure experienced by a day trader is not comparable to that of a long-term investor. The latter does not constantly examine his stock market portfolio. He rarely worries about his investments. In contrast, a day trader is constantly under pressure. For many, the emotions take control and ruin numerous transactions. The best technician in the world has fewer chances of making a profit than a professional trader who has full control of his emotions.

Avoid Emotional Pitfalls

Avoid discussion forums where most of the people are there only to pump up their stocks without using any graphs or information to support their claims. Ignore interventions such as "Go Apple Go!" or "My friend told me that this stock is going to explode!" or "Netflix is going to $900 by Halloween!" These interventions do not help your investment strategy, and nothing is better than the research you can do. Use Twitter or StockTwits and make a list of the best traders on the web. Block access to clowns who provide no content or those who are simply pumping their stocks. You can recognize them quickly.

Moreover, avoid being under unnecessary pressure by becoming the guru of a colleague or a friend. Otherwise, you will suffer from the fear of disappointing those who trust you. Imagine the face of your friend after a 20% decrease in a stock you had recommended. Avoid this kind of pressure that will ruin your analysis. Avoid buying when the markets are falling. The market is always right, and you will eventually learn it brutally. Avoid the pressure to swim against the tide. Technical analysis is not an exact science. Furthermore, your stock may have the most beautiful upward pattern, but if the market is decreasing, your stock will also drop.

Take Control of Your Emotions

There's no doubt that this chapter is the most important one, even though it does not involve technical analysis. To make a profit in the stock markets, you need to discard emotions. The best way to do so is to develop a plan for each one of your trades. When you are in full trading action, take a moment and ask yourself if your emotions, good or bad, are going to dictate your way of trading.

- Did I buy because I received a scoop, or because I highlighted an excellent entry point by doing a stock analysis?
- Did I identify the levels of support and resistance of the coveted stock? Am I selling in a moment of panic?
- Did I collect information about the stock before buying it?

These simple questions will help you to plan your transactions and will protect you from making foolish decisions. The best traders in the world are primarily methodical investors who have precise productivity objectives.

To understand the different emotions that the beginner investor can go through, let's use a character. We'll call him Mr. Smith. Let's assume a situation similar to the one that many traders go through when they begin. Mr. Smith has no experience in trading but wants to try his luck. He goes to his financial institution to open a brokerage account.

His brother-in-law gives him some advice for beginning in financial markets. Some websites provide the background necessary to be ready to act. After a few days, Mr. Smith decides to take action and makes his first transaction. He invests in a stock proposed by a guru.

After two days, he notes with amazement that the stock already offers a 15% potential gain, thanks to a dazzling increase. He is very excited and can't believe how easy he can make money on the market. Mr. Smith goes through some euphoria. He truly believes that the surge will continue. It is not enough for him. Greed takes control, and he wants more. Subsequently, the stock stagnates and remains in a side corridor for a few days.

Mr. Smith asks himself if he should sell or keep the stock. He becomes worried, uneasy, and can't wait for a new leg up to start. He cannot believe that the increase is already over. The fear of losing a potential gain goes through his mind. Quickly, his stock falls and loses more than 20% just before the close of the markets. He is desperate to see that the situation has changed so radically and decides to wait until the next day to see what happens. He hopes, and he is convinced that a reversal will occur sooner or later. Mistake!

The succeeding day, the stock continues its decline. Hastily, and without thinking during a panic crisis, Mr. Smith gives up and sells his stock with a loss of 35%. Totally discouraged, Mr. Smith is not proud of not having sold shares faster. He drops the market for now, completely stunned by his first experience.

Time goes by. He tries to understand what happened. He starts to follow the market again and doing research on the net to find websites that give good tips. When he spots a financial blog that gives scoops on stocks that have already registered gains of more than 100%, hope comes back.

The Market Cycle of Emotions

Mr. Smith has gone through many emotions that made him lose control of his one and only stock. Sometimes positive, sometimes negative, emotions have taken control of his trading, making it impossible for him to know how to react in an unexpected situation. Take a look at the figure 13.1 that presents the list of emotions lived by a trader, in connection with the four stages of the financial markets presented in **Chapter 3**.

This figure presents the superposition of two illustrations: **Market cycle of emotions** and the **Four stages of the stock market cycle**. This figure shows the relationship between the emotional cycle and the four stages of the stock market cycle. The first one shows emotions lived by the traders, in connection with the bullish and bearish cycles of a share presented in the lower part.

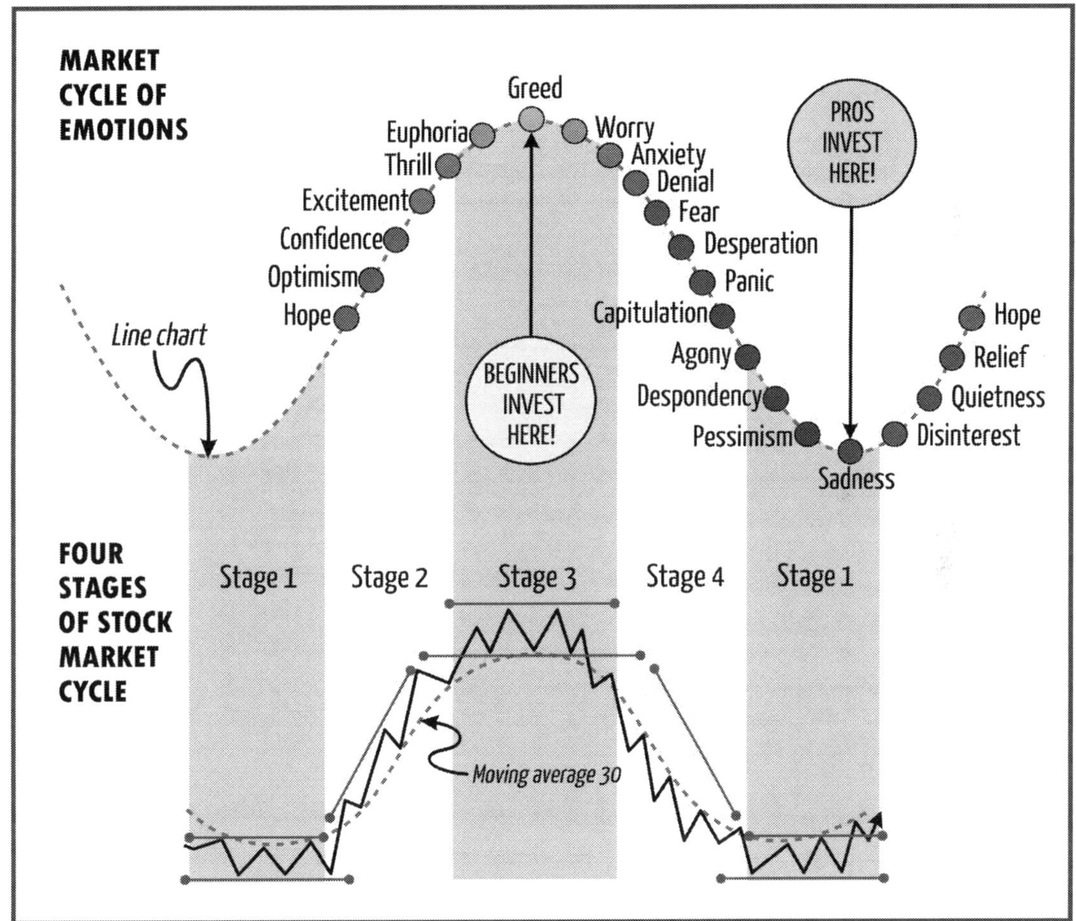

Figure 13.1: Market Cycle of Emotions vs. Four Stages of the Stock Market Cycle

This list is not exhaustive; it just gives an overview of the emotional cycles. Furthermore, observe that the time to invest is completely opposite whether you are a professional trader or a newbie stock picker. Professionals buy when the beginner is set to sell. The beginner is ready to buy when the professional is ready to get out.

Be Disciplined

The best technical analysis is worthless when discipline and rigor are missing from your trading style. Stick to your initial plan and avoid the traps set by the financial community. Determine support and resistance lines to predict future events better. Learn to anticipate reversals. Stop being excessive! Remove from your vocabulary the words euphoria, greed, fear, and hope. Replace them with more pragmatic terms such as analysis, plan or method.

You must be disciplined in performing your technical analysis as well as during the purchase of your stocks. Learn to limit your goals. Bet on small profits on a steady basis. Learn to cut short and take your losses. Admit your mistakes quickly and move on to another transaction. When the market is going through a bad period, the best option is to stay away.

When you have full control of your trading system, stay in a familiar field. Don't try new experiences. If you are successful, continue to work in the same type of market stocks. Be consistent; the small and frequent gains will shape your trading style. Forget gains of 15–25%. Base your strategy on real objectives.

Chapter 14 – Analysis of a Stock

Now is the time to get down to business: technical analysis of a stock. It's essential to make a first analysis of the stock in a weekly format. Why? The weekly chart makes it easier to identify the stages of the stock. As we have mentioned earlier, it's best to focus on stocks that are at stage 2 and, even better, at the beginning of stage 2.

You have to think like the masters who do not hesitate to sell at the approach of resistance. Novices hope for a breakout that probably will not happen, at least not sooner. The chart configurations are unlimited. With some experience, you will develop your own configurations. It is crucial to use many indicators from the four families of indicators seen in the previous chapters. Make sure you are using at least one per family.

Weekly Chart Settings

Here is one of the configurations used to maximize your selection of stocks. Feel free to use other indicators to confirm some divergences. It is practically impossible to obtain perfect coordination between all the indicators. However, for each indicator, we present the parameters and triggering elements to meet.

Indicators	Settings	Triggering Factors
EMA	13	The trends of the stock and the EMA13 are upward.
EMA	34	The trends of the stock and the EMA34 are upward. The crossing of the (fast) EMA13 above the (slow) EMA34 triggers the buy signal.
ADX	14	Favor an upward +DI that has just crossed the 20 level.
Parabolic SAR	0.02,0.2	The trend is upward, and the SAR indicator is below the stock price.
MACD	12,26,9	Favor an upward MACD with bullish crossing above the zero level.
Full Stochastic	14,7,7	Favor a stochastic that had reached a bottom, which has returned upward and has just crossed the 20 level.
RSI	14	Favor an RSI that had reached a bottom, which has returned upward and has just crossed the 30 level.
Bollinger bands	20,2	Favor the Bollinger bands that have been in contraction mode for several weeks and are now about to expand.
Acc/Dist		Favor an Accumulation/Distribution that had reached a bottom and has returned upward.
Volume	30 weeks MA	Favor stocks whose average volume at 30 weeks is more than a million shares exchanged.

Figure 14.1: Weekly settings

How to Analyze a Weekly Chart

Draw trend lines, support and resistance. Identify the bottleneck areas and the future points of sale. Identify patterns and divergences on the chart. Favor only entries at the beginning of stage 2. Don't forget that weekly stage 2 can last several weeks or even months.

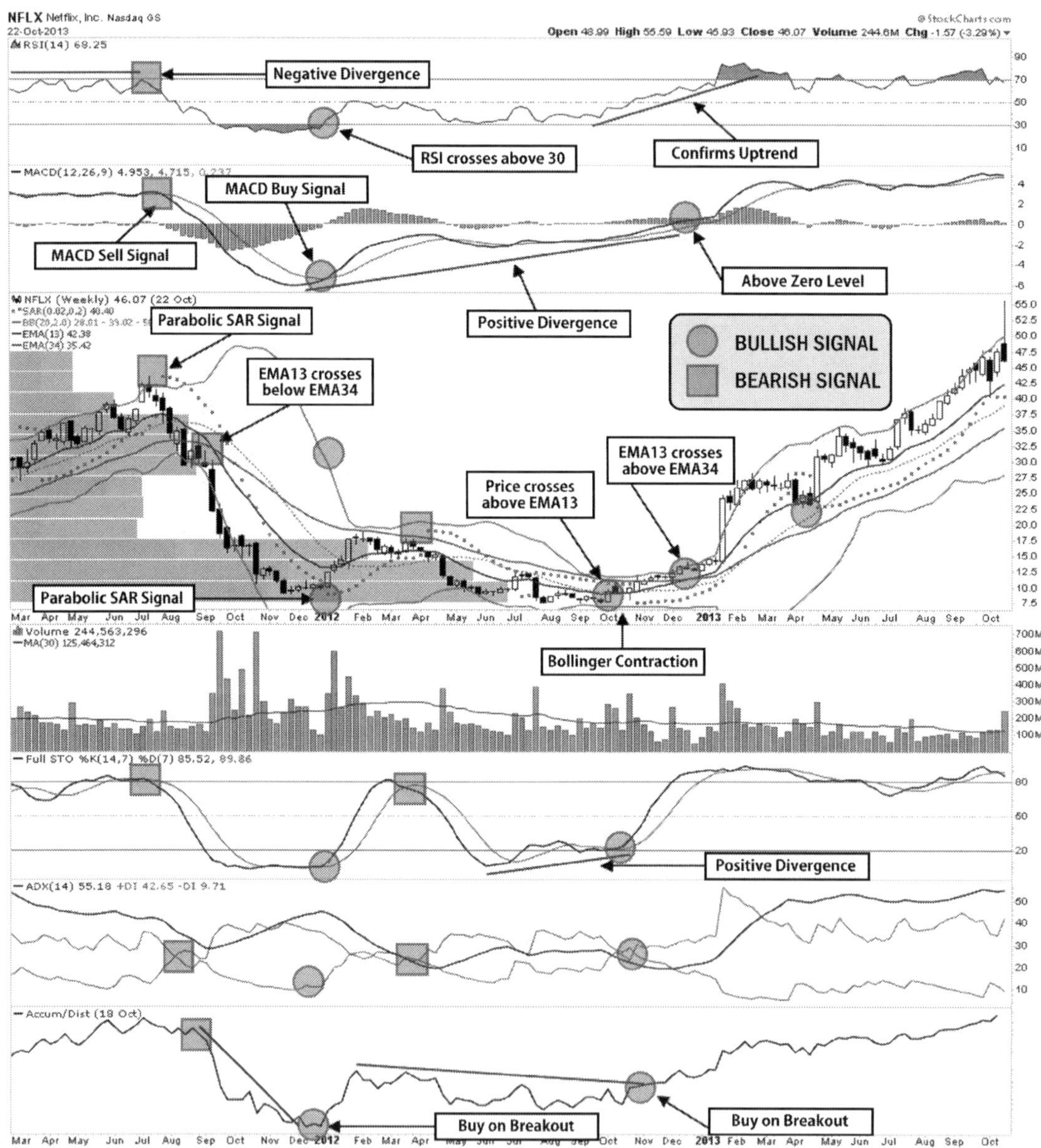

Figure 14.2: Weekly setup

Daily Chart Settings

Here is one of the configurations of daily charts. The analysis of the daily chart has only been useful in confirming the purchase already announced by the weekly chart.

Indicators	Settings	Triggering Factors
EMA	5	The trends of the stock and the EMA5 are upward.
EMA	13	The trends of the stock and the EMA13 are upward.
EMA	34	The crossing of the (fast) EMA13 above the (slow) EMA34 triggers the buy signal.
MA	50	The trend of the stock and the MA50 are upward. It represents a support zone for many investors during an increase.
MA	200	The MA200 is flattened or in a slight ascent. The very high gaps between the EMA13 and the MA200 remain unsustainable. A trend reversal is more than possible.
ADX	14	Pay attention to the trend reversal signal.
MACD	12,26,9	Pay attention to the trend reversal signal.
Full Stochastic	14,3,3	Pay attention at overbought and divergence signals.
RSI	14	Pay attention at overbought and divergence signals.
Bollinger bands	20,2	Favor the stocks on which Bollinger bands are in contraction mode for several days and are about to widen.
Volume	30 days MA	Pay attention to the divergences between the stock price and volume. A drop in volume under the 30-day average indicates that buyers have lost enthusiasm for this stock.

Figure 14.3: Daily settings

How to Analyze a Daily Chart

When comparing a daily chart with a weekly chart, notice that a buy signal (crossing of the EMA13 and the EMA34) is generated much earlier on the daily chart. There is a delay in the weekly signal compared to the signal generated by the daily chart. This is quite reasonable. If you convert an EMA13 and an EMA34 from a weekly to a daily format, you will obtain an EMA65 and an EMA170. Use these parameters on a daily chart. The crossing occurs in the same week as on the weekly chart when using an EMA13 and an EMA34.

The weekly chart served mainly to get a 'prepare to buy' signal. The daily chart is used to confirm the buy signal but will also serve to get a sell signal. Draw trend lines, the support and resistance. Identify the bottleneck areas and the future sell points. Identify the patterns and divergences on the daily chart. From now on, you must check the conduct of your stock on the daily chart every day and spot the signs of weakness that could lead to the need of selling the share.

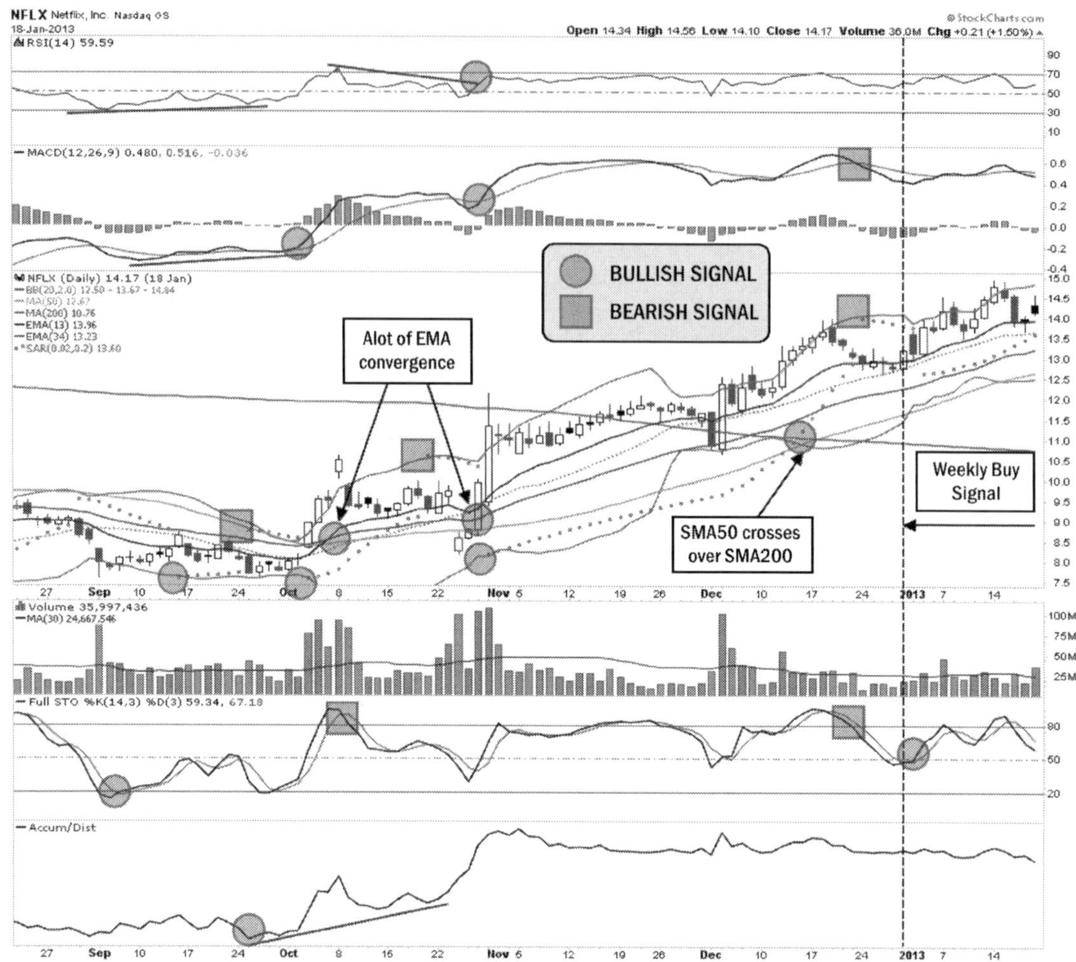

Figure 14.4: Daily Setup

The figure above shows Netflix stock in a daily format. As you can see, many buy signals in daily setups were generated before the weekly signal, identified by the vertical dashed line. This is quite normal since the periods in a daily format (days) are shorter than the periods in a weekly format (weeks). However, the weekly signals often have a longer duration.

The weekly signal is confirmed by a daily signal that happens at the same time. Observe that the weekly signal appears at an exchange rate of $13.25, while the first daily signal was triggered at $9.50. Do not hesitate to sell the stock on signs of weakness. Limit your performance goals. Small daily earnings will bring tremendous growth to your assets.

Chapter 15 – An Upward Day

To understand how the day goes by in the stock markets, we'll use the intra-day chart of Twitter. Volumes are strong. Every day, several million shares are being exchanged. The chart shows very well the ups and downs of a trading day. It is similar for many available stocks, regardless of the industry. A typical trading day is split into four different periods. Let us look at each of them.

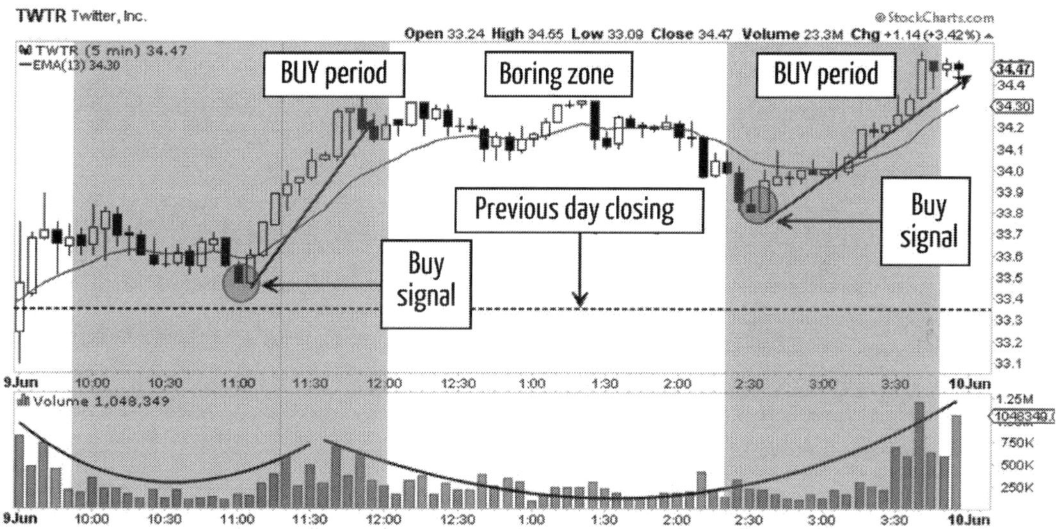

Figure 15.1: Intraday chart of Twitter

Period 1. The Morning attack.

This period is the most volatile of all. Quite often, the upward pressure is so high that it forms a gap at the opening of the markets. The increase continues in the first half-hour. All orders accumulated during the night are being executed. This time favors a significant increase in the volume exchanged. The highest gains are obtained during this short period. Gains varying from 2% to 5% are quite common, prompting traders to position the day before. Subsequently, the stock drops because the pros are cashing quickly their profits. Experience will teach you that a pro has little patience and takes profits rapidly.

Period 2. Buy Zone.

The second period begins when the pullback is complete and lasts until the midday pause. This period still overflows with activity. This is the best time of the day to buy a stock. You will rarely swim against the tide because you bought cheaply.

Period 3. Boring Zone.

Most of this period happens during the lunch hour. Many traders take a small break. Market makers are meeting to prepare the game plan for the afternoon. This zone is the least volatile of the day, with a much lower volume. This period is less attractive and offers a lesser possibility of gains.

Period 4. Buy Zone.

This last period is particularly interesting for taking positions. Many stocks were ending the day well and will start with a bang the next day. This period can favor an increase in volume and volatility. Get used to moving yourself to the end of the day and enjoying the momentum. Unless there's bad news, the stock should open strongly the next day.

As you know, keeping a stock overnight can turn into a nightmare. Stay away from this strategy if you don't like that. If you don't accept this kind of risk, day trading is for you. There are many forms of trading. Whatever your method, the important thing is to obtain positive results.

Chapter 16 – Stock Market Gurus

Here is the big question: "Who is a stock market guru?" The word 'guru' is often associated with those prophets who claim to speak in the name of God. They attract many of the faithful on Sunday morning. Similarly, the stock market guru is a financial visionary capable of detecting efficient shares. In our case, he is a specialist in stock-picking.

This type of guru is widespread on social networks. Cyberspace has permitted the emergence of many pseudo-specialists that offer their stock picks. Many sell their choice against an annual subscription, and others do it for free. Often, gurus hope to attract attention so that the wave of subscribers can influence the market.

Choosing a Guru

As in sports, work or hobbies, many people need to have a person by their side who they can learn from or a master who can reassure them when they're making decisions. It is the same for investment. Most people know nothing about investments and trust their bankers to help them choose the optimum investment. For many people, the best investment will be a bank deposit paying an interest rate of 1%.

Don't mix up financial consultants working in a bank or brokerage firm with the guru specialist in selecting securities. The guru knows the financial markets well, and he has a flair for good picks. He works freely and is not forced to follow guidelines that may go against his values.

Be careful because you are easily attracted by the hope of quick profits. Avoid at all costs the gurus who only recommend investing in penny stocks. Penny stocks are even traded for fractions of a cent. They are often the target of promoters and manipulators. A promoter can create numerous websites whose mission will be to provide recommendations on the same financial stock and give the illusion that it is a future winner.

A simple trick: access your Twitter account, use the search tool and type the acronym of the targeted penny stock. After a few attempts, you will find that different members have exactly the same list of recommendations. Their objective is to attract as many people as possible and catch some fish. Many websites offer free recommendations for financial stocks.

At first glance, this seems interesting. All you have to do is to provide an email address. Why provide an email address? Because they will take the opportunity to sell your address to other sites that work in the Pump-and-dump world. There is no reason to provide your email address in order to get free services. Protect your personal information and your privacy.

Other gurus will provide their picks for a monthly or annual subscription. The subscription costs between $500 and $1,500 yearly. Daily selections are available in several ways: a website, by email, SMS, Twitter or Facebook. The guru's choices will be ready for use before the daily opening of markets. It will be up to you to select the best of their choices.

Be Cautious About Gurus

Your most difficult task will be to find the best guru to fit your trading style and your aspirations. If you believe you've found a rare pearl, try the service for one month only. This will allow you to get an idea about the picks and information available. You will get an excellent overview of the returns it can get.

The selections of your guru must be supported by stock charts. This is a key element. Anyone can present himself as a stock market specialist and provides buy or sell recommendations. Those who support their picks by documented graphics have an edge over others. These professionals understand the importance of presenting picks supported by tangible elements such as technical indicators, bullish and bearish patterns, support and resistance lines, and divergences.

It will take a few days to see the quality of your guru's advice. Is his trading style fine with you? Does he sell stocks immediately after he recommends buying them? Does he buy on short or long term? Does he know the companies he recommended well? Does he make picks that follow the trend of the markets?

Don't take the gurus who make 15–20 recommendations per day too seriously. How are you supposed to make the right choice among all their proposals? How do you track stocks with so many options? Don't trust this kind of guru. You must validate the proposed suggestions to avoid falling into traps. Logically, we like to invest in the stocks that have upward configurations with potential for a few days. Hence the importance of knowing how to analyze securities.

CONCLUSION

Technical analysis is a fascinating world, but the management of all these tools remains complex. In fact, there is no need to master all the technical indicators perfectly. Avoid overburdening your graphs unnecessarily; three or four indicators should be enough. Add to this, the plots of support and resistance lines and the estimation of entry and exit points. Instead, focus on your favorite indicators that suit your style and trading philosophy.

Stay on the lookout for economic news and competition within a business sector; they will have an important influence on the price evolution of your shares. Analysis of your graphics will evolve at the same level as moving or adding support and resistance areas. The course of an action changes over time; it is the same observation for the analysis of its chart.

I sincerely hope that this book will allow new investors to take control of their investments. Stop blindly trusting the advice of others and pay attention to the signals generated by the financial charts. Although the graphics cannot predict the future, it's still the only tangible support available. Avoid the pitfalls of stock markets. The best deal may be the one you do not do.

The distortion in the markets does not help the average investor to make wise decisions. Everything seems to go too fast. Take the time to support your buying and selling decisions. What stage is the stock in currently? What is the trend of the stock? Confirm the buy and sell signals using several indicators to obtain a consensus. Improve the quality of your scans to get a choice of well-established companies that generate profits. Eliminate companies that are traded on secondary markets.

Be on the lookout for new technology trends. Sectors like cryptology and bitcoin will allow the emergence of several companies that will offer spectacular stock market returns. Diversify your portfolio to secure your investments.

I wish you the best of luck!

Charles G. Koonitz

GLOSSARY

Accumulation	The period in which informed traders buy (accumulate) stocks.
Accumulation Zone	A rectangular-shaped formation produced when insiders and investors purchase shares. The chart is characterized by small price movement but relatively strong volume.
Bear Correction	A temporary price retracement in a declining market.
Bearish	Negative stock market sentiment when prices are primarily declining.
Bearish Divergence	A bearish divergence occurs when the price and the technical indicator move in opposite directions: the security makes higher highs, but the indicator is making lower highs. Bearish divergence signals a near-term turning point in the trend.
Bear Trap	Sends a signal that the rising trend of a stock has reversed when it has not. Instead of declining further, the stock price stays flat or becomes bullish.
Blow off	The final phase of an uptrend with a sharp price increase, followed by a sharp decline.
Blue Chip Stock	Refers to a well-known public company that delivers high-quality earnings and have solid fundamentals.
Breakdown	The breaking of a downward trend. The point at which the stock price breaks out of support zone. A falling price below a support level.
Breakout	The breaking of an upward trend. The point at which the stock price breaks out of resistance zone. A rising price above a resistance level.
Bullish	Positive stock market sentiment when prices are primarily rising.
Bullish Divergence	A bullish divergence occurs when the price and the technical indicator move in opposite directions: the security makes lower lows, but the indicator is making higher lows. Bullish divergence signals a near-term turning point in the trend.
Bull Trap	Sends a signal that the falling trend of a stock has reversed when it has not. Instead of increasing further, the stock price stays flat or becomes bearish.
Buy Signal	Represents a good time to buy a stock, triggered by some indicators.
Buying on Margin	Buying on margin is borrowing money from a broker to purchase an asset.
Channel	An area where the price of a stock bounces up and down its support and resistance levels.
Closing the Gap	Consists to close the range where there is no transaction caused by a gap down or a gap up. It could take a lot of periods to fill a gap.
Commodities	Commodities are basic goods that come out of the earth such as wheat, cattle, soybeans, corn, oranges, gold, uranium, copper, aluminum, coal, cotton, and oil.

Continuation Pattern	Patterns that lead to the continuation of the existing trend. Some of the most trusted patterns are: Ascending triangle, Bull flag, Bullish pennant, Cup-and-handle, Rounding bottom.
Consolidation	A zone where a stock trades within limited trading range without much movement. Neither the bulls nor the bears can predict when a stock will breakout or breakdown.
Contrarian	An investor who invests against the crowd.
Correction	A move in a stock which is opposite to the primary trend but not sufficient to alter the primary trend.
Crossover	A point on a chart where a stock price intersects the line of an indicator like SMA or EMA. It could be a crossover between two indicators.
Daily Range	Represents the difference between the day's high and the same day's low.
Death Cross	A point where the 50-day moving average line crosses below the 200-day moving average line.
Distribution	The period in which informed traders sell (distribute) stocks.
Doji	A pattern in a candlestick chart that represents a small trading range. A doji represents an indecision in the market.
Downtrend	A downward movement of a stock price when successive highs are lower than the previous highs and successive lows are lower than the previous lows.
Fibonacci	Ratios used to identify potential reversal zones based on the Fibonacci sequence (1, 2, 3, 5, 8, 13, 21, 34, 55, 89, 144, . . .) and the Golden Ratio at 1.618.
Flag	A chart pattern that shows a flagpole holding a pattern encompassed by two parallel lines. The flag is a continuation pattern that marks a pause before the continuation of the primary trend.
Fundamental Analysis	The study of a company's health and performance that helps investors identify the long-term performance. This is the best way to compare company with competition and sector.
Gaps	Gaps are spaces left on the bar chart or candlestick chart where no trading has taken place. A gap up is formed when the lowest price on a trading day is higher than the highest high of the previous day. This is a sign of market strength. A gap down is formed when the highest price on a day is lower than the lowest price of the previous day. This is a sign of market weakness.
Golden Cross	A point where the 50-day moving average line crosses above the 200-day moving average line.
Index	A group of stocks used as a reference by financial markets.
Ichimoku Cloud	A versatile indicator used to represent price movements; it identifies trend direction and provides areas of support and resistance. Also called the clouds charting method.

Indicator	A tool that uses sets of algorithms that aids in predicting the current or future trend of a stock. (Bollinger bands, MACD, RSI)
Market Cycle	A serie of bull and bearish phases.
Morning Attack	A large buy or sell in the first 30 minutes of a trading day.
Money Flow	Shows the relationship between cash flow towards a stock and its price.
Neckline	Refers to the support or resistance level on a Head-and-shoulders pattern.
Oscillator	An indicator that shows overbought and oversold condition for any stock.
Overbought	When an indicator reaches an upper level, chances are that price has risen too far. A sell-off could start soon.
Oversold	When an indicator reaches a lower level, chances are that price has dropped too far. The security is due for an upward movement.
Pennant	Pattern that shows price ranges that narrows down through a decreasing channel. A pennant is a continuation pattern that marks a pause before a breakout.
Pivot Points	An indicator that determines key support and resistance levels. Pivot points are useful in determining entry and exit points.
Price/Earnings Ratio	The price-to-earnings ratio (P/E ratio) is measured by dividing the price of a stock by the company earnings per share.
Price Patterns	Figure that appears on candlestick charts and that has predictive value like an uptrend, a downtrend or a divergence.
Pullback	A significant short-term reversal in the price of a stock which drops back down after a nice run.
Pump-and-Dump	A form of fraud that involves artificially inflating the price of a stock through false and misleading positive statements on social media in order to sell the stock at a higher price.
Rally	A significant short-term reversal in the price of a stock which rises after a period of decline.
Resistance	A higher level where the stock price could hit during the surge of a stock. A lot of sellers will slow or even reverse the uptrend.
Retracement	A reversal in the price of a stock. Becomes popular with the tool Fibonacci retracement that shows possible reversal points of a stock price.
Reversal	A trend that is moving back in the opposite direction.
Reversal Pattern	Patterns that lead to a change in the direction of a stock price away from the current trend. Some of the most trusted patterns are: Double bottom and double top, Falling wedge and rising wedge, Head-and-shoulders bottom and head-and-shoulders top.
Sector	Represents a group of companies that produce and sell the same kind of products.

Sell Signal	Represents a good time to sell a stock, triggered by some indicators.
Short Selling	Short selling is the sale of a security that is not owned by the seller or that the seller has borrowed in the hope that the price will go down.
Support	A lower level where the stock price could hit during the decline of a stock. A lot of buyers will slow or even reverse the downward trend.
Trading Range	Spread between the high and low prices traded during a period of time.
Trend	The directional movement of a stock price.
Uptrend	An upward movement of a stock price when successive highs are higher than the previous highs and successive lows are higher than the previous lows.
Volatility	A measurement of change in market price over a given period and the comparison to historical values. Volatility measures the risk of a security.
Volume	The number of shares traded on a stock exchange during a period of time.

BIBLIOGRAPHY

TECHNICAL ANALYSIS BOOKS

Ichimoku Charting & Technical Analysis - *The Visual Guide for Beginners to Spot the Trend Before Trading Stocks, Cryptocurrency and Forex using Strategies that Work*, Tripod Solutions, 133 pages, 2019.

Trading Psychology in the Zone - *How to Understand the Cycle of Market Emotions and Use Technical Analysis to Make a Profitable Trading Plan*, Tripod Solutions, 81 pages, 2018.

Technical Analysis for Beginners Part One - *Stop Blindly Following Stock Picks of Wall Street's Gurus and Learn Technical Analysis* (Third edition), Tripod Solutions, 123 pages, 2018.

Technical Analysis for Beginners Part Two - *Riding the Stock Market Cycle (Second edition),* Tripod Solutions, 125 pages, 2018.

Trading Strategies in the Zone - Profiting from Technical Analysis and Bullish Patterns, Tripod Solutions, 105 pages, 2018.

Technical Analysis for Beginners - *A Practical Guide for Charting,* Tripod Solutions, 215 pages, 2018. (Paperback version of Technical Analysis Part One and Part Two)

SELF-PUBLISHING BOOKS

Ebook Cover Design for Self-Publishers - *Create an Attractive Look Using Color,* Typography, Pictures and Cover Design Concepts, Tripod Solutions, 158 pages, 2017.

99 Formatting Tips for Nonfiction eBooks - *How to Format a Better eBook Using Various Tips on Cover Design, HTML, Typography, Images, Layout, Conversion and Testing,* Tripod Solutions, 197 pages, 2017.

Kindle Formatting and Publishing like a Pro - *80 Self-Publishing Mistakes Explained, Tripod Solutions,* 194 pages, 2017.

INDEX

A

Accumulation/Distribution 45
Ascending Triangle 60
Average Directional Index ADX 36
Average True Range 48

B

Bar Chart 8
Bearish 13
Bearish Divergence 22
Bearish Engulfing 82
Bearish Harami 86
Bollinger Bands 47
Breakdown 14
Breakout 14
Bullish 13
Bullish Engulfing 82
Bullish Harami 86
Bump and Run Reversal 70
Buy Signal 17

C

Candlestick Chart 8
Candlesticks Patterns 81
Chaikin Money Flow 41
Channel 20
Consolidation 13
Continuation Pattern 57
Crossing Moving Averages 31
Crossover 34
Cup and Handle 57

D

Dark Cloud Cover 84
Day Trading 41
Dead-Cat Bounce 58
Descending Triangle 62
Distribution 45
Divergence 21
Doji 81
Double Bottom 72
Double Top 73
Downtrend 15
Dragonfly Doji 87

E

Evening Star 85
Exponential Moving Average EMA 14

F

Falling Wedge 66
Fibonacci 31
Flag 63
Force Index 38

G

Gravestone Doji 87

H

Hammer 83
Hanging Man 83
Harami 86
Head-and-Shoulders Bottom 74
Head-and-Shoulders Top 75
Horizontal Line 32

I

Indicator 21

L

Line Chart 8
Long-Legged Doji 81

M

MACD 29
Market Cycle 13
Market Cycle of Emotions 97
Momentum 15
Momentum Indicators 41
Morning attack 103
Morning Star 85
Moving Average 13

N

Neckline 58

O

On Balance Volume 55
Overbought 41
Oversold 41

P

Parabolic Rise 78
Parabolic SAR 37
Pennant 63
Piercing Line 84
Pullback 35
Pump-and-Dump 11

R

Rally 14
Rate of Change ROC 44
Relative Strength Index RSI 41
Resistance 13
Retracement 89
Reversal Pattern 69
Rising Wedge 67
Rounding Bottom 77

S

Sell Signal 31
Short Selling 55
Simple Moving Average SMA 29
Stochastic 41
Stop Loss Order 27
Support 7
Symmetrical Triangle 63

T

Technical Analysis ix
Trading Psychology 95
Trading Range 20
Traps 89
Trend 7, 13
Trend Indicators 29
Trend Line 15
Triangle 60

U

Uptrend 16

V

Volatility 14
Volatility Indicators 47
Volume 13
Volume by Price 53

Made in the USA
Columbia, SC
13 October 2021